COUNTER-DESECRATION

Edited by Linda Russo
and Marthe Reed

COUNTER-
DESECRATION

A Glossary for Writing
within the Anthropocene

Wesleyan University Press | Middletown, Connecticut

Wesleyan University Press
Middletown CT 06459
www.wesleyan.edu/wespress
© 2018 Wesleyan University Press
Manufactured in the United States of America
Designed by Mindy Basinger Hill
Typeset in Minion Pro

Library of Congress Cataloging-in-Publication Data
available upon request

Hardcover ISBN: 978-0-8195-7845-7
Paperback ISBN: 978-0-8195-7846-4
Ebook ISBN: 978-0-8195-7847-1

5   4   3   2   1

To indigenous peoples, to peoples of island nations
and the Sundarbans imminently imperiled,
and to all other beings suffering in the Anthropocene

tó

        tó

        tó

        tó

        tó

        tó

        tó

        tó*

Sherwin Bitsui | "*tó*"
*Navajo for "water"

CONTENTS

PREFACE

This glossary delivers terminological impression of shifts in language and in consciousness fostered to address the perilous state of today. Continually fed now since Euro-invasion, intentional attempts at extinction/slaughter of the Western Hemisphere's indigenous peoples (estimates say that 75 to more than 100 million people rapidly perished at the hands of the Euro-invader and his diseases) undoubtedly spurred the initial methane surge of the Anthropocene. This is, immediate and dire, an enduring era of environmental injustice, survivance under unequal protection from colonial, imperial resourcing, with political sabotage by collective lessening of efforts to combat climate change. Now, in the Sixth Extinction epoch segment, we strive to locate lingual succinctness in attending to the multitudinous expression with participatory means to discern and disseminate information necessary to better the state of the world for all peoples and all lives dependent on our shared planet. Moreover, we strive to employ as vernacular this nomenclature and vocabulary in idiolect of intentional lexicon while gathering activist effort for gross intervention, reclamation, renewal, revivance, and restoration, by whatever means necessary to keep this world inhabitable and whole beyond what damage has already diminished its complete viability.

In imagining a book that would clarify the new ways that we respond to the call our earth, her oceans, and the surrounding atmosphere surely sing, *Counter-Desecration* brings sustenance and power with terms made in collective remedying. From *dysoptics* to *echolocution*, *reciproesis* to *terrotic*, the countenance of communication encounters the need of a global population on its mettle. *Torpor* (the rest state required of an activist) and *vivitocracy* (a social mind-set built on the idea that all life deserves equally to exist) bring a sense that our collective strength and support of the planet might still replenish and recover her ability to continue, and thus we along with her, or at least give a sense of the hope for future life here. This book allows us fortitude and wisdom to secure what means we might to continue to cherish and to equip us to protect our planet with concise and meritorious language and action: a generous undertaking for which I am exceptionally grateful and believe indispensable for writers, speakers, readers, and researchers working for vital cause and solution.

ACKNOWLEDGMENTS

LINDA RUSSO: A testament to the beautiful, fierce, generous heart of Marthe Reed, this book is dedicated to her memory. I wouldn't have wanted to do it without you, Marthe. Thank you Allison Adelle Hedge Coke for your powerful preface. Thank you Christine Leclerc and Brenda Iijima for curatorial assistance, and thank you Julia Bloch, the editor of *Jacket2* who unwittingly provided the forum to commence this project. Finally, I wish to thank, always, my family, for sustaining (with) me in many ways.

MARTHE REED: Gratitude to Linda Russo for imagining this project, to our contributors whose collaboration gave vision form, and to Mike, who makes everything possible.

ENTANGLED & WORLDLY

Approaches to Anthropocene Writing

Without deep reflection, we have taken on the story of endings, assumed
the story of extinction, and have believed that it is the certain outcome of
our presence here. From this position, fear, bereavement, and denial keep
us in the state of estrangement from our natural connection to the land.
Linda Hogan | "Creations"

In a substantially altered world, when sea-level rise has . . . made cities
like Kolkata, New York, and Bangkok uninhabitable, when readers and
museum-goers turn to the art and literature of our time, will they not
look, first and most urgently, for traces and portents of the altered world
of their inheritance? And when they fail to find them, what should they—
what can they—do other than to conclude that ours was a time when
most forms of art and literature were drawn into modes of concealment
that prevented people from recognizing the realities of their plight? Quite
possibly, then, this era, which so congratulates itself on its self-awareness,
will come to be known as the time of the Great Derangement.
Amitav Ghosh | *The Great Derangement: Climate Change and the Unthinkable*

Staying with the trouble requires making oddkin; that is, we require each
other in unexpected collaborations and combinations, in hot compost
piles. We become-with each other or not at all. That kind of material
semiotics is always situated, someplace and not no place, entangled and
worldly. Alone, in our separate kinds of expertise and experience, we

know both too much and too little, and so we succumb to despair or to hope, and neither is a sensible attitude.

Donna Haraway | *Staying with the Trouble*

Over twenty years ago, Linda Hogan's essay "Creations" clarified a need for "new terms and conditions that are relevant to the love of land, a new narrative that would imagine another way."[1] Many have lived another way, many have imagined, many have faltered, and many have not: the narrative of advancement at any cost remains dominant, and here we are. Given what we know, how will, and can, we respond? Will we resist, with Hogan, the story of endings? Confront, with Amitav Ghosh, what it will take to avoid the Great Derangement? Override despair, with Donna Haraway, by creating new ways to stay with the trouble? The purpose of this glossary is to provoke possibilities for responsive writing within the Anthropocene, as defined both by the ongoing machinery of the carbon-fueled economy of late capitalism and the corresponding disruptions to planetary systems, and the corresponding disruptions to economic and social orders, and the corresponding reexamination and adjustment of those orders, and so on. It proposes that approaching any place as actively shaped and bearing social and environmental histories of wildness and settlement is one way to begin to respond. It further proposes that anyone can embed themselves in the sites and corresponding ecological systems that we modify for dwelling, preserve as wilderness, or cultivate for profit around the globe, engage pressing questions, generate new methods of inquiry, report back on the state of our living world(s).

We come across key words that help us understand our relationship to what we know and try to know. We invent these words for each other to use, or we repurpose them, keeping language vital.

Counter-Desecration: A Glossary for Writing within the Anthropocene is a collection of such words—words that can act as keys to thinking and acting in our lived place-times because they engage cultural, economic, and social framings that determine ecological relationships. Regardless of the debates surrounding the term *Anthropocene* within and across disciplines, the discussions advance and new descriptors proliferate—*Capitaloscene, Capitalobscene, Misanthropocene*—further emphasizing the need for vital writing. Donna Haraway's *Chthulucene*, to my mind, speaks most directly to the ground and possibility of making. Joining *khthôn* (beings of earth) and *kainos* (now, fresh, new), it names "a kind of time-place for learning to stay with the trouble of living and dying in response-ability on a damaged earth" and suggests that, as chthonic ones, we can "demonstrate and perform the material meaningfulness of earth processes and critters . . . [and] also demonstrate and perform consequences."[2] Entangled and worldly: we are all somewhere and each connected to myriad life-forms. Can we write response-ably, responsively, to our time and places as a way of remaking where (and how) we find ourselves?

The most powerful words jostle frameworks, unsettling and enabling shifts of understanding, use, and contexts. For those interested in protecting natural environments, Robert Macfarlane's *Landmarks*, a collection of glossaries for the British Isles, marked a significant moment. Macfarlane set out to stop the destruction of places whose life and reason we cannot see and as a result drew attention to a hunger for words that can sharpen our knowledge of places. *Landmarks* gathers geographically specific words in dozens of languages and dialects that reflect "waves of invasion, settlement and immigration"[3] to enable familiarity with places we (do and don't) inhabit according to the logics of the primary constituents of those places—plants, animals, minerals, and weather cycles that make life possible. Macfarlane cites as a precedent the grassroots effort to detail the life of a brindled moorland on the Isle of Lewis in the Scottish Hebrides that was being targeted by a British energy company.[4] Learning their home was an ideal site for a massive wind farm, local poets and artists responded by making narrative, poetic, painterly, photographic, historical, cartographical, and lexical accounts, including Finlay MacLeod's "Some Lewis Moorland Terms: A Peat Glossary."[5] This collaborative labor represented the "barren" landscape as a living habitat and clarified how individuals specializing in profiting from natural resources had failed to value the landscapes that provide those very resources. That the energy installation proposal was defeated speaks volumes about the importance of the knowledge(s), so foreign to industry, that poets and artists work with and create. It shows how, through acts of progressive world-making, new or forgotten concepts (re)emerge. It is this kind of (re)emergence, a becoming-with, that *Counter-Desecration* hopes to inspire.

Macfarlane found inspiration in Barry Lopez's *Home Ground: Language for an American Landscape*. Both of these books provide crucial information for landscape literacy and emphasize the value of accurate, and where possible indigenous, place-based knowledge. Both gather language that "keeps us from slipping off into abstract space"[6] — words that help us make *something* of landscapes that would otherwise be perceived as "developable" *nothings*. Further, both books celebrate *national* landscapes. As Lopez elaborates, acquaintance with a language that helps one say "more clearly and precisely what we mean" would

> draw us closer to the landscapes upon which we originally and
> hopefully founded our democratic arrangements for governing
> ourselves, our system of social organization, and our enterprise in

economics. If we could speak more accurately, more evocatively, more familiarly about the physical places we occupy, perhaps we could speak more penetratingly, more insightfully, more compassionately, about the flaws in these various systems which, we regularly assert, we wish to address and make better.[7]

It is in this relational overlap—between places and the human systems and practices that shape them, between our flaws *and* our desires—that *Counter-Desecration* focuses. It takes up the lens of geographical humanism, seeing places not as empty containers but as fields of relations already constituted by multiple trajectories of myriad beings, each bearing their social and environmental histories. At the same time, it allows us to ask who is *our*? and what is *ours*? For coming to terms with this, too, is another urgency posed by the Anthropocene. When powerful individuals and organizations choose to ignore the reality and risks of climate change, by, for example, hampering and censoring the work of scientists, we must continue to utilize and invent ways to see what we need to see.

Home Ground was published in 2006, and while some of its entries address natural resource and land use issues, the US-Mexico border, and global warming, reading geography for signs of human dominance was not a primary goal. In *Counter-Desecration*, by contrast, some of *Home Ground*'s lexicon reappears, rendered anew. For instance, *game trail* differs from "trail" by citing big animals (elk, bear, etc.), "our first civic planners"; *The Great Plaints* redefines "plains" by singing a lament of species displacement; *south border- land* amplifies ideologically driven violence as a defining feature of a "borderland"; and *watershed* emphasizes our fluid relationship with earth's water by detailing toxic presences, such as heavy metals, pesticides, and pharmaceuticals. The inclusion of common terms is not by design, but it emphasizes place as semantically active and knowledge of geographical features as critical for grasping effects of the Anthropocene.

The story of conflicting visions for Lewis's brindled moorland resonates with current conflicts in the American West over cattle grazing, dam removal, fossil fuel extraction, wolf populations, and suburban development and habitat and biodiversity maintenance (currently, survival of the sage-grouse is at stake). The same anthropocentric perception that often guides energy infrastructure developments—that there is "nothing" out there—affects grasslands and river ecosystems, myriad species, including humans; NoDAPL (No Dakota Access Pipeline) and other front lines in the pipeline resistance continue to make this clear. The story of the moor also resonates with my own becoming-Anthropocene story, of growing up in a northern suburb of New York in a home bordered with trees and surrounded by town and state parks and Nature Centers. The apparent consistency of these "natural" contexts obscured the causes and effects of actual changes: housing developments eating up huge swaths of woodlands and pastures, a state park originally named for indigenous people renamed for a US president, a wetland filled in to build a shopping mall. Eventually I'd realize how I'd learned how to see-not-see. In "The Place, the Region, and the Commons," Gary Snyder warns that "the world of culture and nature, which is actual, is almost a shadow world now, and the insubstantial world of political and rarefied economies is what passes for reality."[8] The degradation of actual worlds and spaces is not in any sense a uniquely American phenomenon, but Americans continue to follow the mandate to approach places with dollar signs blinkering our eyes.[9] Economic growth trumps rights to a safe and healthy environment, especially those of marginalized, poor communities located in industrial or increasingly industrialized zones. And this movement doesn't stop at our borders, as we are expert at outsourcing accumulated trash and toxic labor, sending plastics and computer components to Asia to be "recycled," for example. In other ways, the force of dominant power structures shapes places and relations in our ecological present. These include, but are not limited to, structural racisms and colonialisms that threaten civil rights; practices of "development," from agriculture to energy infrastructure to housing, that influence human settlement and fragment habitats and destroy biodiversity; toxic legacies of industries, such as mining, that make development on these scales possible; and policies that exacerbate the effects of mounting climate instabilities (floods and landslides, melting glaciers and shrinking coastlines, droughts and forest fires). Add to these the fact that acts of economic and ecological violence, whether causes or effects, are inflicted on the most vulnerable, and the consequences, deemed externalities, are often ignored or made invisible, especially to those of us located in the global North. All places change, and the remaking of places, it seems, always comes at a cost, but the nature and rate of that change depend on our ability to articulate what (besides capital) is being exchanged and how we and others will be affected. The bioregional knowledge derived from indigenous people who have a long history and culture of living in a place without destroying it is vital, as is access to knowledge necessary to comprehending the ideologies and mechanisms of the advancing projects that culminated in "the Anthropocene."

"The Great Derangement" is Ghosh's name for a fictional retrospective labeling of our current age, when "most forms of art and literature were drawn into modes of concealment that prevented people from recognizing the realities of their plight"[10] — that is, that we live in a world already substantially altered by, and destined to experience the cataclysmic results of, climate change. Ghosh traces a history through the Enlightenment to arrive at a contemporary situation in which literary works by and large maintain the "partitioning" (Bruno Latour's term) of "Nature" and "Culture" that consigns science exclusively to the former, while forbidding literature, as works of "Culture," to address science, thus leaving a gap in inquiry and knowledge. Ghosh blames this partitioning for the "suppression of hybrids" like science fiction (which he himself writes). In recent years, many works of creative nonfiction have addressed this gap by engaging current frameworks of scientific knowledge and popularizing the lexicons of botany, forestry, ichthyology, microbiology, and ornithology, for example, as evidenced in these titles published in 2016: biologist Hope Jahren's *Lab Girl*; two works by naturalists, Richard Mabey's *The Cabaret of Plants* and Stephen Buchmann's *The Reason for Flowers*; German forester Peter Wohlleben's *The Hidden Life of Trees* and Fiona Stafford's *The Long, Long Life of Trees*; Jonathan Balcombe's *What a Fish Knows* and Sy Montgomery's *The Soul of an Octopus*; David Montgomery and Anne Bikle's *The Hidden Half of Nature*; and Jennifer Ackerman's *The Genius of Birds* and Jonathan Balcombe's and Leigh Calvez's *The Hidden Lives of Owls*. That we live in an age of inspired attention to the "hidden" truths of other species on earth is evident. This is also the age of the sixth extinction. If we *are* coming to grips with how little we know about what we are losing, shall we then do more to challenge destructive narratives of progress that rule our age?

This, according to anthropologist Anna Tsing, is an absolute necessity because our stories for moving into the future rely on dreams of modernization and fail to "address the imaginative challenge of living without those handrails, which once made us think we knew, collectively, where we were going"[11] —toward a singular, improved future. Our condition is one more of precarity than of certainty, and our survival may depend on our ability to embrace this, on our willingness to abandon visions of organization made stable through either harmony or conquest and "emerge in blasted landscapes"[12] — to live with our messes together. This is a good place to pause and consider the possibility presented in *Counter-Desecration*. Poets, Ghosh acknowledges, were always at the forefront of the resistance to modernity's "partitioning." And so this glossary, a hybrid and a collection of hybrids, proposes to inhabit and enliven the realm of literary thinking about science and philosophy, racism, colonialism and anticolonialism, politics and geography. Poetry is a marginal art both because it works the edges of thought, suturing discourses and inviting strange bedfellows, and because it pushes thinking away from popular, conceded-to topics by entering new terrain. *Counter-Desecration* hopes to inspire a poetic resurgence through the creation of new contexts for realization and enacting life-affirming change.[13]

The fact that, for Tsing, survival will be collaborative corresponds with the collaborative nature of this glossary. We wanted to know others' ways of seeing, and what others were creating or had come upon and remade for their own use.[14] Perhaps to give the whole venture the air of legitimacy, we proposed to collect what we called "entries." But what contributors wrote, in addition to pieces that would fit (for the most part comfortably) in a standard language reference text, were narratives, poems, lists, manifestos, meditations, and microessays. The terms themselves reflect the various ways of experiencing and putting language to places and the systems with which we interact. Many entries move edgewise into that complexity, to disrupt powerful, globally invested corporate myths that efface particularities of emplacement and of myriad, diverse realities. Many entries are place-based or write from an embodied perspective; others bear implications for emplaced thinking. Glossary contributors draw on a range of heritages and knowledges, including those from Asia and the Pacific Islands, along with those more prevalent in the global North. They draw on a diversity of landscapes, from wilderness to suburban, from urban to rural, from mainland to island. They draw on history, philosophy, and scientific, political, and literary theory; on research, fieldwork, and creative praxis; on experiences rare and unique and mundane. Together they create and re-create mobile, shifting fields of inquiry. Each entry begins to tell a story, because the violent erasures of complexity that define the Anthropocene force us to provide our stories of who we in any place are, what we in any place value, and how in any place we enact who we are and what we value.

Many of these words and their entries will seem weird. As Haraway points out, the urgencies of this era "demand that kind of thinking beyond inherited categories and capacities, in homely and concrete ways."[15] This brings to mind the concept of *enchantment*, the active, self-directing, entry into interrelational complexity that depends on a willful suspension of certainty or already-knowing. Or, more simply put, the return to wonder. Macfarlane hoped for a "Counter-Desecration Phrasebook," a "glossary of enchantment for the whole earth, which would allow nature to talk back and would help us to listen."[16] In the Anthropocene, with nature shouting new realities, I propose we think of enchantment as what transpires when, with our most capable depths, we listen. Enchantment gives us a way to *engage*, to approach and grapple with a thing through its difference from us, its difference from our archive of ideas about it, and allows us to grasp what it means to give things the dignity of their names. Under the spell of enchantment, writing can work against the erosion of the significance of the too easily ignored, because lowly (*that* weed, *that* trash heap), pathetic (*that* endangered mammal, *that* marginalized human), or scaled beyond our ability to reason (*that* melting glacier, *that* toxic landscape, *that* sacred mound, *that* unfamiliar, powerful, life-affirming cultural practice).

Counter-Desecration treats words as portals to new species of wisdom. It draws on and hopes to nourish our capacity to continue to discover and know ourselves anew as we venture beyond inherited, ingrained categories. Some terms, including *communicate, echolocution,* and *reciproesis,* provoke new forms of listening. Others, including *archipelago, protector,* and *use without using,* confront biological and cultural losses inflicted through colonialisms and suggest strategies of resistance. Others work at the ground level to prompt intimacy with places or to clarify modes of *detourning* dominant or destructive forces, as in *akiw8gon, bluestoning,* and *echoherence.* Still others prompt further understanding of the other-than-human world (*phytosentience, shadow, weave watching*). Some lay bare and/or propose alternatives to operative frameworks of late capitalism, such as *biotariat, ecobereavement,* and *ovulept;* such frameworks are always wrought through historical entanglements, as highlighted in *IOYAIENE, negative corpuscuity,* and *phylogeny.* Some, such as *betweenness, Radical Indigenous Queer Feminist,* and *torpor,* allow diagnosis or identification; others, action, as in *making, nomensuture, protext.* And there are those that prompt us to question what we mean by "our" and "selves." *Air* cites "poetry's (literal) *inspiration*" and suggests, "Best to write in open air or beside an open window to foster feral connection with earth's atmosphere, other beings, and our human capacity for sensory situatedness"; *crypto-animist activism* offers guidance for "communicating with or being aware of nonhuman objects, creatures or presences during such direct actions as civil disobedience"; *dispersal* may apply to "the self [dispersed] into decentered relationship with other living organisms by instances of beauty."

What and who falls under the category of "ecopoetry" and whether "ecopoetics" is or is not a "movement"—these things are currently debated. *Anthropocene writing* is our preferred term because it downplays the tendency for categorizing and instead emphasizes the act of writing and the unifying fact of the times we live in. Accordingly, *Counter-Desecration* includes contributors of many aesthetic dispositions, just as the entries derive from various modes of writing and inhabitance and reflect a range of political responses. We reached out to poets because we believe they have a unique role to play. Poems can instantly question, break open, and reorganize thinking and produce new understandings and affiliations. Poems can work on a scale that enables one to quickly enter into, if only imaginatively, the consequences of our perceptions of, and our hopes for, our attended-to realities. Walt Whitman suggested as much when he wrote of departing from the lecture by the learned astronomer to look up at the stars, and much contemporary ecopoetries engage this concept, from expansive poems like Allison Adelle Hedge Coke's "The Change" or Juliana Spahr's "Gentle Now, Don't Add to Heartache" to more incisive poems such as W. S. Merwin's "For a Coming Extinction" or Ed Roberson's "be careful." The adaptive capacity of poetic form gives this genre currency.

In Haraway's "we become-with each other or not at all" I hear echoes of Heraclitus's "thinking is the thing that links all things." When we think, we always *think with*. When we act, we always *act with*. This glossary provides concepts to think and act *with* and suggests ways to embed thinking and action. Prioritizing poesis, its lexicon is both *material* and *motive* for writing. The contributors have invented entries that highlight mode, affective and responsive capacity, and context. Please consider using these entries as poetry prompts, though they weren't written as such. What these entries *do* prompt is seizing the power of one's embeddedness within systems that make one feel *least* powerful. They don't retreat from the structural residues of historical events that (sometimes by design) fail to recognize (or disregard) the needs and desires of the individual. In fact, they acknowledge these as part of our contemporary condition. It's quite possible that, offered *as* prompts, these entries will *obstruct* the goal of completing a poem as such. In a very ordinary way, these entries may encourage one to set aside thinking of the poem as an outcome of (prompted) writing, and engage writing instead *in relation to*, located within, what's at hand, what presents in the field of inquiry any individual may create. This glossary is guided by roomy questions like *How do we write through the unanswered present and/or future needs and desires of individuals, cultures, landscapes, and their human and nonhuman inhabitants?*[17] *How do we respond to aspects of the sum total of earth culture?* Honestly, I don't know if it provides answers. It provides methods, ways to explore, and it invites reworkings of these methods. It may provoke one into unpredictable encounters, which are always the most transformational. If, as Charles Olson wrote, "conditions are what we are all inside of," this is a book (an unfinished book) of conditions. After all, the ability to generate methods for responding to aspects of the sum total of earth culture *are what we have.*

As an example of the inventive power of contemporary poets, *Counter-Desecration: A Glossary for Writing within the Anthropocene* hopes to generate new ideas about our relational, expressive, creative capacity as humans encountering the devastating effects of the dominating ideologies of our era. At the very least, it draws attention to what may otherwise remain unacknowledged. Each term prompts us to ask how we learn, and teach each other, to see, how we respond to the obstacles we detect in our ways of seeing, and how we can nurture positive shifts in relations between ourselves and others, the places we inhabit, and the forces that shape them. I hope the words provide for the reader a sense of why to pause, where to turn one's creative and intellectual energies, how to take even the smallest first steps. While we may feel immobilized by senses of grief and helplessness that seem to be vying to define our era (cf. *Anthropocene Anxiety Disorder*), we are agents of change amid changing agencies, and when we connect our small efforts and realizations to other small efforts and realizations, we are doing something to create the world we choose to live in. And even if all one can do in their poem is signify their human being-there and living-amid our conditions, we may, to cite Anne Waldman "leave a trace so that poets of the future know we were not just slaughtering one another."[18]

Notes

1. Linda Hogan, *Dwellings: A Spiritual History of the Living World* (Simon & Schuster, 1995), 94.

2. Donna Haraway, *Staying with the Trouble* (Duke University Press, 2016), 2.

3. Robert Macfarlane, *Landmarks* (Penguin Random House, 2016), 8.

4. For further details, see Macfarlane, *Landmarks*, 27ff.

5. The phrase "Counter-Desecration Phrasebook" is credited, by Macfarlane, to MacLeod; the *Peat Glossary*, a kernel text for Macfarlane's *Landmarks*, listed over one hundred Gaelic words and phrases, drawn from the local populace, for describing this landscape in detail—words like *caochan*, "a slender moor-stream obscured by vegetation such that it is virtually hidden from sight."

6. Barry Lopez, ed., *Home Ground: Language for an American Landscape* (Trinity University Press, 2010), xxiii.

7. Lopez, *Home Ground*, xvii.

8. Gary Snyder, *The Gary Snyder Reader* (Counterpoint, 1999), 192.

9. The process of exchanging the actual for the insubstantial is glaringly visible in the events that unfolded since 2006, when a "Donald J. Trump State Park" sign sprung up on an escarpment overlooking the Taconic State Parkway after one well-known developer's plans for a golf resort

failed. Today the grounds contain the plowed-under ruins of an early twentieth-century estate—decaying buildings, dilapidated tennis court and swimming pool—an unmaintained "gift" to the State of New York, sold inexpensively on the condition that it bear the businessman's name.

10. Amitav Ghosh, *The Great Derangement: Climate Change and the Unthinkable* (University of Chicago Press, 2017), 11.

11. Anna Lowenhaupt Tsing, *The Mushroom at the End of the World* (Princeton University Press, 2015), 2.

12. Tsing, *The Mushroom at the End of the World*, 3.

13. The analogy, borrowed from Tsing, is to the ecological process of resurgence, which is the ability of plants and animals to move around and make their own rearrangements of and contributions to an ecosystem in the wake of any quick disturbances, such as farming or deforestation.

14. This project commenced in June 2015, with entries by eighteen contributors, titled "Place-Relation Ecopoetics: A Collective Glossary"; it was the final entry in my "Emplaced and local to" commentary for *Jacket2*. The online launch of this project, I now know, coincided with the development of other Anthropocene glossaries in various fields, from individuals involved in anthropology and international climate institutes, for instance.

15. Haraway, *Staying with the Trouble*, 7.

16. Macfarlane, *Landmarks*, 32.

17. In this question I hear echoes of a Native American ethic toward seven future generations.

18. Anne Waldman, *The Iovis Trilogy* (Coffee House, 2012), 656.

ENTRIES

air: a little song, a poem. English lute airs were particularly popular in the early modern era (see Thomas Campion's *Two Bookes of Ayres*).

—what invisibly passes through bodies, like wind through an aeolian harp, creating song. *And what if all of animated nature / Be but organic Harps diversely framed* (Samuel Taylor Coleridge, "The Eolian Harp").

—what is exchanged by living things (in the troposphere or dissolved in water).

—a medium carrying smell and sound. *Rose is a rose is a rose is a rose* (Gertrude Stein, "Sacred Emily").

—according to the World Health Organization, air pollution caused approximately one in eight global deaths in 2012, making it the "world's largest single environmental health risk."

—poetry's (literal) *inspiration*. Best to write in open air or beside an open window to foster feral connection with earth's atmosphere, other beings, and our human capacity for sensory situatedness.

að jökla (International Phonetic Alphabet: ä:ð̩ jœkʰļɐ): the neologism *að jökla* takes an Icelandic verb form and applies it to the word for glacier (*jökull*). This follows the behavior of Icelandic seasonal verbs such as *að vora* (to become spring) and *að vetra* (to become winter), signaling metamorphic transition as their action. The glacier-verb neologism traces transition; in the case of current usage, it implies a flux in mass, leaning heavily toward transitional disappearance. The creation of this action word also allows for empathetic embodiment of glacier experiences. Encouraged as a loanword to languages outwith Icelandic.

akiw8gon (the *8* is pronounced like the French *on*) is from the Abenaki word for "Land," "Aki," and our basic concept of continual process, *w8gon*. *Akiw8gon* is the continual becoming of the *Land*, and we people as part of that ongoingness. *Land*, for us, includes not only the geographic place, but also all the nonhuman and human people who make up that particular place—including both those things Western culture sees as alive, such as Plants and Animals, and those things that they generally don't see as alive, such as Stone, Mountains, Rivers, Lakes, Clouds. *Land* is a word of intimate relationship. *Akiw8gon* acknowledges the *Land* as a process of becoming in which everything has personhood. Our participation in *akiw8gon* means, first, that we *listen*—that we pay attention with all of our senses, with our bodies, spirits, and our intellect to what is happening, what is becoming now at this moment. See **Land, reciproesis**.

animacy: I hunt in Eduardo Kohn's *How Forests Think: An Anthropology beyond the Human* for the word *animacy* while two mutts sleep at my feet. They bark. We go outside. I see the morning glory has finally bloomed; a white butterfly I do not "identify" visits it too. "Situated, intimate engagement." That's how I sum up these pages from the chapter titled "The Living Thought," which begins with barking dogs followed by a silence—in Quechua: *hau' hau' hau'* then *chun*. The dogs are dead. Prey to a puma. Kohn then unfolds a complex argument: "If thoughts exist beyond the human, then we humans are not the only selves in this world. We, in short, are not the only kinds of *we*. Animism, the attribution of enchantment to these other-than-human loci, is more than belief, an embodied practice, or a foil for our critiques of Western mechanistic representations of nature." I read and take notes so as not to count days: day 32 of the Soberanes Fire; seven days, says the vet, until my oldest dog will die—food itself a toxin for her now. As an always already *we*, we remain a toxin for this planet? I read on, taking notes because Kohn's animacy (or at least his articulation of it) offers possibility.

Anthropocene Anxiety Disorder: a feeling of hopelessness about the future from within the Anthropocene, and a sense of helplessness about doing anything to change the trajectory of the era.

archaeology: dredging up, for example, the shards of drought (broken crockery) set in place this instant centuries ago to salvage the eulogized conduits of empire failing to draw water from plunder; verbiage in muteness; or toxic invisibilities (the new Persephones): not only as discourse, but as corporal ecstasy and fruitful disgust. Scoring in turn such incidents of rupture in the surface of the general text (see still Michel Foucault, *L'archéologie du savoir*).

archipelago: the assured acknowledgment that all islands emit light and all landforms are capable of receiving them. The archipelago acknowledges the dire state the Anthropocene and the peril of rising sea levels portends, and it thus fortifies its knowledge by seeking out other islands beyond its knowing. The notion that other islands have answers, too, buoys the archipelago. For the past many centuries, the various islands of the planet's myriad archipelagos have got on well, despite there being no walls. There is an open invitation for atolled nations to seek out archipelagos. See **atoll**.

archive: a place is an archive of its own ruins. A place is the archive of trauma as fact. It happened here. The ships came by to pick up people, their cargo, and the people hauling cargo. The Pacific is our trauma and our desire. The rim is everywhere there has been a war to get caught up in—always carrying the officer's status in the body—always involved in the closed-door domesticity of empire.

Your daily commute through it, or your tourist visit to it, or your wrong turn leading to it, or your binding obligation to stay in it may be a document of the place's ruin. You can sense the bodies that passed through the place before. Flown above. Eaten tunnels through. Exposed the brick and fuel spills. Paid out. Locked down. The body knows more than the curatorial eye of the drone or the tight porn shot. Or the preservationist's weak references, the developers' biopolitical commitments to life. Ruins and remains post-disaster is a place of present presence, neither passed nor futurist. "Which by now have turned into ruins." "He was there to collect the past."

attention: directed mental, physical, and spiritual awareness. Listening, observation. Also care—attending to a place, time, system, being. Consistently threatened or thwarted by various forms of distraction—devices, tasks—as well as by emotional reactions, including guilt and fear. Can be enlarged, sometimes, through practice, diligence, and carefully chosen tools. See **making**.

atoll (verb): protect, fortify, build up, wall off, confidently proceed with limited knowledge, onward, establish (political) precedence; *atolls* (noun, usually plural): the rapid transformation of a once giving nation into one governed by a latent fear, bred from a presumed, imminent threat. Nation-states in atolls preemptively insulate themselves by building walls of increasing heights. The goal is a state where no one can see out and realize the need to get out, and where no one can see in/come in. See **archipelago**.

azhigwa: now is not a time for grief or silence. the earth spits forth its seeds; new life germinates in even the narrowest crevices. the waters surface and rush. *azhigwa* is to breathe time, to thread one's hands through the atmospheric filaments. there, on the branch. a dissimulation of birds. ask them to tell their story. it is not pretense or deceit to survive a cataclysmic extinction. listen to their songs. this note, how it trills beside the next. azhigwa. we are torqued and bleeding. already. we are alive.

bearing: as in the quality or state of being of import, a notation. A single bird begins geographic fact. The straightest degree begins to be opposite other and everything in declination, negative or west of relative to one's surroundings. A single bird's tiny shift can move the entire flock, an accident of direction or wingfall fall left and right into the space between us and ocean. Index intuition. Weather/whether, where does the bird end and the sky begin? A projection of words between direction between wing and rotating parts, at once open and precise—a biological compass. Words enter forward and shift along lines of magnetic force pushing out a sequence of syllables before the gesture of flight weights position.

betweenness: the space between the house and the forest is the "field," between one shore and the other is the "river," between the rocks and the trees is the "trail," and so on. Mary Louise Pratt's characterization (in *Imperial Eyes*) of the "contact zone" as the activity and dynamics of the site of betweenness for colonial encounters can be usefully applied in other geospatial encounters. I think of that hyphenated space as a "trans-" poetics, a *trait d'union* that acknowledges otherness and difference, movement and stasis. The advantage to standing in the doorway is that you can see both rooms, while also gaining the knowledge of the spaces of resistance, silence, listening. Attention to being "between" is one way to locate the murmur of our intersections with place, that one is somewhere, not everywhere.

betwixtuation: that in the book of *x* its margins are neither edge nor end but the interval between the word and the world. & that in the between there is a kind of weltschmerz (as much a fatigue of form as it is a weariness/wariness of binaries, of either/or) but also the disarming and simultaneously activating power that is nuance. This space/speech sheds a strivingness, sheds austerity's suits/formulas in favor of raw messiness: *this hot mass*: disobedience: *they were literally sitting in the middle of the street reading books en masse*: becomingness: *maybe this is the bardo*: receptivity: *where habit has not yet done its work*: the ghost of an imminent superabundance: *placental, iridescent mystery*. Betwixtuation is the power of encounter, the constant movement of associative, energetic complexities between bodies, the coincident, polytropical possibilities of bearing (carrying, supporting, enduring, giving birth to, intuitive wayfinding) and baring (i.e., flashing, exposing, uncovering) the source. The crux of a betwixtuation is flux.

biotariat: the political "class" appropriate to the Anthropocene, or the era of geophysical capitalism. The idea that, once we can perceive the *total* impact of capitalism on *life itself* (this moment in which *all biological life*—as both "labor" and natural or material "resource"—is exploited for the production of surplus value—to the point at which the entire biosphere faces exhaustion and collapse), just then does it become necessary to develop a new political consciousness and new revolutionary subjectivity *on the basis of life as such*. Hence a reframing of struggles in terms of intersystemic and interspecies responses and responsibilities that recognize "the commons" as a system of ecological sustainability, writ large, into which human social re/production must fit. The proposition of the biotariat calls a new collective identity into being, a new common subjectivity formed by life itself, which we are only beginning to find out how to access and enable agentically.

bluestoning suggests a field of activities contingent on Catskill Mountain sandstone.

investigative bluestoning: following the various thicknesses and shades of blue-gray, cut into rectangles, squares, or patches, that once made up sidewalks from the Hudson Valley to New York City: a country of bluestone sidewalks, like a stationary moving sidewalk (think airport people mover), so some stand and others walk. Sometimes I follow the submerged bluestone to a historic cemetery or a furnace in the woods.

divinatory bluestoning: divination by tossing fragments of this sandstone into the air and reading the future from the spread it makes. Like reading tea leaves in the pits of an abandoned quarries in the Catskill Mountains, and we find in old sites that humans make furniture—tables and thrones—and even rooms in the woods out of this flat layered rock.

bodied: between the said and the unsaid, there we are. Ever-mutable and entangled. You are an archivist of endangered sounds. Pay attention to the memory of your senses, the felt experience of your having been here, there, somewhere, in your body, among others, within time, on this earth. Collect moments like layers of sediment and ash, air, water in the vial of you.

body regionalism arises from bioregional attunement. *Bioregion* (life-place) is a term used to define a place in terms of its life-sustaining systems rather than to ecologically irrelevant political boundaries (such as state and nation). Body regionalism acknowledges all bodies as inclusive of bioregion. If a bioregion is the place where all conduct the business of living at all points along all cycles of organic processes, body regionalism harnesses implicit and explicit reciprocities to extend its possibilities. May be perceived as an affective consequence.

bordered: It's November post-11/9 and I am in Mexico, in a colonia somewhere outside Piedras Negras. A rosebush borders a wire fence in the small yard. Six roses survive . . . perhaps from harsh weather conditions . . . perhaps from thirst . . . the rest have died. Perhaps it's just plain luck that there are still petals blooming like organs bursting out of a fresh cut-open corpse. I watch children run and laugh because perhaps joy is free. I overhear a white woman, an American like me, nearby, reach down and pet a stray dog passing us. She says, to the dog, not the children: You must be so hungry. All you need is some love. I remember when I was in Romania. I still have nightmares about all the starving dogs.

B-RAD (Bio-Regional Attachment Disorder): attachment disorder characterized by dysphoric response to coexistence in biodiverse context with inabilities to dwell in cosmic awareness with creative agency ≈

Treatment: walks ≈ local waterway/woods ≈ naturalist training (see: Birmingham Audubon Mountain Workshop) ≈ hiking ≈ camping ≈ beloved(s) ≈ wildlife (refer to raccoon @ Desoto State Park cabin #8 ≈ fox @ Rickwood Caverns State Park campsite #13) ≈ improvement when power totems & metaphysical agents emerge as vultures, ticks ≈

Cross-reference: "I can't abide what the world has become, the frozen-ness of our product this evil thing that we kiss the ass of every hour. I want a dailiness that is free and beautiful" (Alice Notley).

burrowing (both verb and noun) is a movement (constantly beyond where it just was) of digging deeper than the known, as I've owned it, as I have acquired it and held as ground. Burrowing means *borrowing* from the unknowable, for as long as it will allow it, whatever it will give (no gift is given to be kept). Rather than trying to hold tightly the acquired of my past, I will inquire into burrowing's gift, which might too soon vanish, if I let fear hold me back from the likelihood of falling, which is always inward as well as toward something new, in all its ferocity, even if its gift is a wider glimpse of the void behind anything I reach for, and beneath any ground.

bycatch refers to all species caught that are not the target species, which can be as high as 85–90 percent by weight (as documented in the shrimp trawler fishery in the Gulf of California). We might also regard many of ourselves as bycatch, caught up in systems of global plunder and extraction. The commercial apparatus that is a shrimp trawler is akin to a global economic system that catches so many bodies in its nets, in its slow—and fast—violence. Some of us are better able to survive the nets, some of us have the power or privilege or luck to move away from the nets, but many of us (because of uneven economics, and/or institutionalized racisms, sexisms, speciesisms, and/or xenophobia that plays out geographically) are unable to keep out of the nets. Bycatch, then, is a term that leads to consideration of multispecies environmental justice, witness, and kinship.

clasping: being with the beings and places you're with, setting aside defenses, ego, and fear. Centered on physical presence and proximity, clasping eschews intention and does not work toward outcomes. Origin: clasped hands; the human hand's desire to clasp another hand, or anything handlike. Contrast with *grasping* (being present or approaching presence, but with extractive intent).

climacteric: a critical juncture, menopause, and in botany, a ripening process of increased cellular respiration. Beyond death, more breath, beyond capitalism's logics of labor. As she bounds over the ruins of bounded individualism into the beyond, sweat is still not OK. Or aboriginal peoples exchanging sweat as greeting. "I think too much of my skin — if it wrinkles, blisters, cracks, bubbles, then I am properly attached!" Beware of the too-pure, of eyes too fresh they don't see. Here comes the menopausal whale distributing resources, pod leader, versus young: womb, hoard, death. Throw out your legal rights, autobiographies, and baby supplies! She clears her docket for work as she pleases though not without grief: her friend in poetry in excess of productivity. Tender heart, not breathless, depleted. World as fruit ripening on the vine, death sweetening. "After we think we've killed it, earth will still continue" because the phytoplankton are talking, their invisible-to-the-human-eye tentacles and pillow shapes calling for bacteria to come swimming over, orchestrating the bloom that could cover it up and start again. To connect botany to her body, she climbs up to the last rung, arms full of mantras, potions, and cooling breath because the medical industry is of no use, calling her heightened follicle receptivity a mistake. Life is. Don't worry. Syndrome? Ha! Prisms of electric color spilling out of her mouth. Her belly spills over the edge of her swimsuit as she sits on the beach lounging, balancing that big egg on her knee until it tumbles into the crack, deepening, a brand new hatch.

cloudygenous describes the results of lifestyles and practices resulting from living in the internet so that internet becomes the "place" generating its own indigenous peoples and/or practices.

This could be positive—for example, when the internet facilitates engagement with the universe beyond one's physical borders. This could be negative—for example, when the e-magination of the cloudygenous replaces physical reality and engagement with such reality. It's not an adjective that's inherently negative or positive; it's more complicated, in the way a cloud can obscure but also generate life-supporting rain.

communicate (reciprocal verb): to learn, guide or be led, be led or guided by. To be like the weather, in response. To see a dead squirrel rotting or feel the wind blowing or see a bud swelling or shriveling. If you water a plant, you're communicating with it. When it exhales oxygen that you can inhale, it's communicating with you. Through attention, through care, inadvertently, by accident, through waste. To listen, ask questions, to release your ions, to receive. Also, to inflict: *what* you (collective) communicate matters, charges. To overhear, be overheard. To move in a mass, as birds, ahead of weather.

conspectus: a single viewpoint offering a view of hills and mountains, identified by their place-names. (see **place-name**).
A conspectus is a place where you can thread your eyes in and out of the hills in a narrative sequence, with no fixed starting point or end point. The form frequently eschews summitism; conspectuses are usually located at ancient sites of dwelling—for instance, confluences. Derived from Wittgenstein, the term was first employed by the author in 2010, when he created fourteen mountain conspectus for the Isle of Skye.

crypto-animist activism: the practice of communicating with or being aware of nonhuman objects, creatures, or presences during such direct actions as civil disobedience, strikes, occupations, demonstrations, or other acts of political resistance or risking arrest. Crypto-animist activism considers beetles, finches, flies, moss, dirt, bacteria, foxes, lichen, reeds, or even houseplants within buildings that are having simultaneous existences, whether related or unrelated to human agency or human intentionality. Crypto-animist activism can be practiced every(w)here (see **everyhere**) at any time, whether metaphorically or not, and is a highly effective strategy for focusing on "the untended"; Jonathan Skinner writes that only poetry can "attend to the untended as the untended, essentially leaving it alone" as he asks us to consider weeds in disturbed landscapes ("Thoughts on Things: The Poetics of the Third Landscape"). The practice of crypto-animist activism can be practiced individually, communally, or ritually, as Leslie Marmon Silko notes in "Landscape, History, and Pueblo Imagination": "Survival in any landscape comes down to making the best use of all available resources."

curb cut: any small, subversive action that encourages justice, ecological balance, and local nourishment by cutting into the status quo. When artists embark on works, or people on actions, that they feel are right to do, but about which they wonder, "What difference will this make?," this is a sign that they are undertaking a curb cut. Thus the term invokes discourses surrounding individual versus systemic responses to ecological issues such as climate change. Origin: from the rainwater harvesting practice of making cuts in sidewalk curbs to divert stormwater into infiltration basins (also called rain gardens); the practice reduces flooding, filters water, and nourishes plants.

the deep:
Warmly,
The deep is a downward devotion.

Down here with her, I remove myself from embodying, putting on a different skin. The deep — The Below of Sedna's self-made home. Strength is not easy.

Sedna says:

Come down here and help me with this phantom-pain-turned-animal on my body. I deserve your love down here because I have not deserved any of the traumas I have been dealt.

Descend through the razor-sharp slit, passing beyond the lifeless souls and the hideous cauldron, to her in her own home, sea realm, marine mammalian realm. There is work to be done. They know it, they have come here to do this for her.

Massage her aching, loving her. The "mistress of life and death" needs be courted, appeased, softened by shaman love.

desire line: the way we want to go. often the shortest distance between two points. an expediency. a trampling and then an erosion. an accretion of many subjective individual decisions. pavement-like soil, cracked. outlaw to the prescribed paths of the state or landscape architects. an ever-widening way. in need of care and restoration. the opposite of meandering, an antonym of lost. a microcosm.

dispersal: of seeds by wind, rain splashes, or in the fur or scat of animals, or by theft, especially colonial British; of species uphill in response to climate change; of human experience by language, often metaphor (must we always have one to live by?) or formal experimentation ("the self is a guinea pig" — Leslie Scalapino); of a shifting gaze, which provokes a readiness to move: look back this way, see the . . . ; of the self into decentered relationship with other living organisms by instances of beauty that may lead to fairness (Elaine Scarry); as a rupture, even joy, because "one is several, incomplete, and subject to dispersal" (Lyn Hejinian).

distributed centrality is an ethical value term for the equal centrality of every being, place, and event, recognizing the coconstitutive fluidity of those three forces. On the surface of our planet, the center happens at every point. Such equally distributed value is necessarily nontotalizing and disconnected: nothing is everything, and no one is everyone, in an expanded everywhere. Distributed centrality dismantles competitive judgments that are really about power, such as prize culture and similar reifying exclusions. It's an invitation to be simultaneously at home and away, to value the world's connected dispersals, to act so that the center is a generous everywhere. Distributed centrality emphasizes our ability to recognize the water, the stone, the child, the other, whether or not the other recognizes us. These are human values we write, and their challenges are our conditions. If everything is equally central, the importance of our actions is clear.

ditch: a conduit, often alongside a road or a path, which conducts water, often wastewater, from one place to another. This type of earthwork is constructed to have a single use: conveying water. As with a road, this single use is often flouted or ignored, and the ditch become a garbage dump, a car hazard, a fishing pond, a toxic site of play. As major rain events and catastrophic flooding increase and make much current infrastructure obsolete, the trash, the effluent, and the stagnant water that have always characterized the ditch's promiscuous, opportunistic, and polluted waysideness begin to spill over into the spaces a ditch is intended to drain or skirt. It is a figure of lowliness, and as such is generous (though poisonous) toward those who wish or need to hide. And that's the knack of a ditch: every thou might interact there unobserved. Related natural landforms include the gully, the arroyo, and the damaged spillway.

diversity: what will save us. Interrelations and interdependence between and among the multitude of kinds of species, plants, animals, humans, protect species from danger to reverse rates of extinction. It is nourished by reversing kinds of thinking that devalue diversity. Fostering the spread of diversity in all its forms, difference outdoes homogeneity for greater perspective, expanded ideas, increased empathy; results in a stronger social, ecological, economic weave.

dysoptics: a strategy of destructive rhetoric by which a speaker claims things to be much worse than they are, in order to habituate the targeted audience to the further degradation of said things. Dysoptical claims prepare the way for the intentional ruination, dismantling, or elimination of environments, social programs, regulatory agencies, or any opposing viewpoint. A subcategory of dysoptics reverses this technique, insisting things are fine when they are not, and denying all evidence to the contrary (e.g., climate change denial). Dysoptics seeks to distort perception and can be especially effective when combined with nostalgic appeals to a golden past, extravagant promises of a vastly improved future, or some combination thereof (e.g., "Make America Great Again"). See **nomensuture**.

earth: to bring (a person) to (the) earth. To cost the earth. Earth almond. Earth art. Earth artist. Earth auger. Earth bag. Earth-baking. Earth-bank. Earth-based. Earth bath. Earth battery. Earth-bedded. Earth-beetle. Earthbind. Earth-bird. Earth-blinded. Earth-bob. Earth-bottom. Earth-bred. Earth-built. Earth-burrower. Earth car. Earth chestnut. Earth-child. Earth closet. Earth coal. Earth connection. Earth-conscious. Earth-convulsing. Earth-creeping. Earth current. Earth dam. Earth-damp. Earth day. Earth-delving. Earth-destroying. Earth-devouring. Earth-dimmed. Earth dog.

Earth-drake. Earth-eating. Earth-ejected. Earth-embracing. Earth-fed. Earth-flea. Earth-flea-beetle. Earth-floored. Earthflow. Earth fly. Earth-foam. Earth-fold. Earth fork. Earth-friendly. Earth girl. Earth-glacier. Earth god. Earth goddess. Earth-hauling. Earth history. Earth hog. Earth-holder. Earth-hole. Earth hut. Earth-incinerating. Earth inductor. Earth ivy. Earth lead. Earth leakage. Earth life. Earth-line. Earth loop. Earth-lord. Earth-louse. Earth-made. Earth-magic. Earth-maker. Earth-measure. Earth-measuring. Earth-moon. Earthmoss. Earth-mound. Earth-mouse. Earth movement. Earth-noise. Earth of alum. Earth of vitriol. Earth-oil. Earth orbit. Earth-orbiting. Earth pea. Earth-piercing. Earth-pig. Earth pigment. Earth pillar. Earth plane. Earth-planet. Earth plate. Earth-pole. Earth-power. Earth-puff. Earth-refreshing. Earth resistance. Earth-rind. Earth-roofed. Earth-rooted. Earth sack. Earths-amazing. Earth satellite. Earth-scraper. Earth sculpture. Earth-sheltered. Earth sheltering. Earth shock. Earth-shrew. Earth shrinkage. Earth sign. Earthslide. Earthslip. Earth-smell. Earth-smelling. Earth smoke. Earth soul. Earth-spider. Earth spike. Earth spirit. Earth spring. Earth-sprung. Earth-squirrel. Earth-stained. Earth station. Earth-subduer. Earth-surface. Earth table. Earth-threatening. Earth throe. Earth tilting. Earth time. Earth-tint. Also calling to (the) Earth. Earth to Earth. Earth-tone. Earth tongue. Earth-treading. Earth tremor. Earth-turned. Earth-vexing. Earth-wall. Earth-walled. Earth waller. Earth wave. Earth wax. Earth-wheeling. Earth white. Earth-wide. Earth wolf. Earth-worker. Earth-worn. Earth worship. Earth-year. The ends (also end) of (the) earth. To feel the earth move. To go to earth. To lose earth. To make the earth move.

echoherence: logical or biological interconnection seen through a lens of ecological situatedness. Example: She leaned on a larch, and the shadow cast by the two was an echoherence.

echolocution points toward an ecological writing practice grounded in active listening techniques and attends to its formal qualities through the incorporation of material elements from the soundscapes in which the writing is present. Reflecting the presence of the many environments writing may inhabit—in its composition and/or its performance—echolocution also emphasizes awareness and active incorporation of silence into the work—as a contrasting element to the poetic and nonpoetic sonic events, and as a material entity in itself. Silence decentralizes writing, allowing the emergence of the soundscape to quietly insist on its necessary presence for such an ecological poetic practice.

ecobereavement: I think of how wrecked, how orange and cream, Delhi is when I drive across it, the pollution like an inverted dome in which a person in front of you could stumble and what you would notice first is the seam of crimson blood at their temple, an emphasis of the thickening air around them. An ornament. A brooch. To mourn or grieve in the mode of ecobereavement, describe the burnt verge, the spool of cloth you lie down on. This is the asphalt of the capital. A makeshift memorial. For whom or what? But you're not thinking these things in the instant before you yourself kneel then lie down. Don't get up. Nobody sees you lying there; you can smell the shit on the soles of their shoes as they walk past. In this scenario, you're a woman from a nonnative, nonwhite background. You're the weirdest kind of tourist there is. Ecobereavement: are the suicide rates of farmers in Karnataka, Tamil Nadu, Haryana, Punjab, and West Bengal a marker of this, as winter falls?

eco-justice poetry exists at the intersection of ecology and social justice and culture. Aligned with environmental justice thought and activism, inspired by the "17 Principles of Environmental Justice" developed by the first National People of Color Environmental Leadership Summit, with the knowledge that racism, colonization, and economic injustice lie at the heart of environmental crisis, eco-justice poetry seeks to decolonize our ecopoetry. Eco-justice poetry recognizes the human right of all people to self-determination and the right to enjoy a healthy life-sustaining environment, free from harm. We recognize the role of culture in creating human bonds with the environment and the role of poetry in preserving culture. We value cultural diversity and bring it to the forefront of ecopoetry, celebrating the diverse cultural traditions that feed ecological thought and poetry.

ecolyric: *eco-*, from *oikos* (Greek), meaning "family," "property," "household"; *lyric* (adj.), pertaining to the lyre, or characteristic of song. Also, poetry that expresses feelings. Thus, *ecolyric* (adj./n.): pertaining to feelings of home, expressed musically. Songs of earth and commons.

But what happens to your songs if the home of which you sing is depleted, contaminated, colonized, or absent? How do you sing of home if you are in migration, forced transport, or exile; if you are detained, displaced, deported, or dispersed? What if your home does not support or extend your form of life—your traditions and knowledges, gender expression, sexuality, attachments—and enable you to move and thrive? What if your home makes you sick?

Brenda Hillman wrote that as people continue to cause environmental harm, lyric does not sing "comforting ditties"; instead, "lyric is rendered on torn, damaged, or twisted strings." Today ecolyrics are songs of species loss, drought, disaster, toxic burden, attrition. Ecolyric is elegiac, choral, polyvocal, interrupt-ed/-ive, allusive, collaged, curated, composted, translative. It is document, artifact,

dirge, trace. Ecolyrics are also songs of resistance, refusal, exten-
sion, and restoration. They demand recognition, remediation, and
responsibility.

ecopoethos: a neologism of three roots, *eco, poesis,* and *ethos,* pos-
iting a "household" disposition, wherein *oikos* has neither border
nor limit and *disposition* denotes ethical relation (akin to Gary
Snyder's *earth house hold*): both creation and creative mode. Yi
Fu Tuan's description of *topophilia*—"The affective bond between
people and place"—arising out of "experiences mostly fleeting and
undramatic, repeated day after day over a span of years" and Ed-
ward Casey's idea of *implacement* in landscape painting—the per-
son observing the landscape "integral" to it, rather than outside—
are foundational to *ecopoethos*. When habitation moves beyond a
passive residence on a particular ground to ethical relationship via
the topophilic sense, being, making, and ethical relation become
integrated.

empiricism: nostalgia based on what *was* observed; a remem-
brance of things past
    memory's simile: it was *like* this
    *(jellyfish shapeshifted like strange dreams in the sea; the monarchs
used to tack themselves to this tree, yes this one, like fragile scraps of
orange silk until it seemed ablaze with torch song; once you saw a
whooping crane rising to flight in the white static of spring snow—
white into white, flash of scarlet cap—like a resurrected mythology)*
    in a sentence: as disaster capitalism plunders the remnants of its
late empire, empiricism emerges as a desperate tenderness
    prehistoric pangolins—golden scales like artichoke leaves, a rub-
bery pink noodle of a tongue—carried into the African bush by the
Pangolin Men, who protect them from poachers

do-over by genetic de-extinction: 4.2 million cryovials of tissue samples stored in a Smithsonian biorepository

reflowering: nearly 1 million seeds dreaming in the Arctic Circle's Doomsday Vault;

Japanese robo-bees that can pollinate flowers, made from tiny drones, horsehair, and a sticky ion gel, like that uncanny whirring and persistent ticking of hope—or is it hubris?—stirring the coal-polluted sludge of our long-since-mechanized hearts.

everyhere arises when any*where* is considered a vital "here" through a situated affective human attentiveness. Describes both a multitude of such dispositions (in many *heres*) and the possibility of invoking multiple subjectivities in a vital *here* (hence "everyhere," as opposed to "anyhere"). Corresponds with poetic embeddedness or embodied poesis. Continuous with a range of healing gestures.

game trail: animal trails wind through almost all wild landscapes. Meanwhile, about every road in North America that fits the lay of the land—that follows a river or valley, links woodland townships, heads into the hills, or winds up a mountain pass—was first laid down by big animals. Gridwork neighborhoods and long federal highways are the main exceptions.

That road that takes you to a lake or river? Deer, elk, moose, coyote, bear, or cougar took it first. They cut tracks through the brush and knew the best way through the hills: when "the bear went over the mountain," he probably took an established route. Trackers and hunters, then doctors, gamblers, traders, and people looking for lovers, walked along tracks laid down millennia earlier. Eventually came horses, carts, wagons. When the automobile arrived it too traveled "the old ways."

Ghost herds of fauna, our first civic planners. Let's call roads game trails for a while. It might be instructive to get a book on animal tracks. To study it is to see a world that lies beneath our own.

geohaptics (*geo*: relating to the earth; *haptics*: relating to the sense of touch) describes the extreme intimacy of ecological entanglement, via the air, water, and matter we take in and continually re-become. The nature of this contact is closer than any other as it touches the body at every moment and level of interpenetration with "the environment" (and therefore the impossibility of being disconnected or estranged from it at all). Akin to Tennyson's description of God as "closer . . . than breathing, and nearer than hands and feet" (oft cited by Timothy Morton) and e. e. cummings's description of his lover "whose most frail gesture are things which enclose me, / or which i cannot touch because they are too near," this *too-near-ness* might also describe where geohaptics soften and move through borders of discrete or individual bodies or substances—through pores, cell walls, alveoli, mucus membranes, sense organs, and so on.

geopathy: Earth feels everything we do.

geopoetics: from the Greek: *geo* (earth) and *poesis* (making). Literally, earth-making. Critical human geography helps one think about scale. Geopoetics might be mulch or compost or the building of earthworks to collect stormwater runoff and plant the rain in the desert. Consider land art, new environmental art, permaculture practices, gardening. Or consider the Anthropocene and climate change as geopoesis—and hence, to return to scale, geopoetics is a means to consider appropriate technology and political ecology, and poetry is technology as well. A "quest for wiser ways of dwelling," wrote Anne Buttimer. "What we're concerned with is a new world-sensation," wrote Kenneth White. Also, speculative more-than-human geopoetics: a reflective and refractive earth-making that imagines and speculates on alter-subjectivities.

The Great Plaints [plaint, *n.*, roots ME *playnthe*, ME *plaunt*, pre-seventeenth century *plante*]: plant haunting. Conjured by uneven ecotones (echotones) carved out by homestead plows. Litany *. . . bluestem tumblegrass purpletop needleandthread buffalograss western wheatgrass switchgrass mannagrass salt grass wildrye squirreltail threadleaf sedge . . .* lamenting mass displacement of native prairie grasses, agricultural succession of soybean and feedlot corn. Ghost flora—toothed or hollow-throated—projecting auricles, pollen grains fossilized in sediment. Purple, blue, green, gold, straw, many-brown, black-voiced—plain to ungulate and glire.

horhizome: 1. the visible *différant* by which relation may be traced ("The health of the eye seems to demand a horizon"—Ralph Waldo Emerson). Yet not sky, not beyond, but the foreground seen as the beginning. From the ground, roots and branches, logic of resemblance spreading from no center to no boundary, things as seen signets distributed equally/unequally in boundless space ("barnstorm, boom, boost, bulldoze/pan out, splurge"—Ronald Johnson, *Ark*). From the microphage mesh to the farthest planet, horhizome expresses the intersystemic homology of the ecoverse. 2. Conversely, the unseen horizon of centerless relation. Provisional, in flux, indeterminant, processural, the unseen view, or prospect of, near/far, above/below, leaping, neaping, noding. Viz Timothy Morton, and the ecological thought "a vast, sprawling mesh of interconnection without a definite center or edge. It is radical intimacy, coexistence with other beings, sentient and otherwise." Horhizome traces the node's node, the mesh enacted in a "quick graph" (Philip Whalen), consciousness stitching relations in scale, above/below, seen/unseen.

improvement: as used to settler-*colonize* and resource-*dispossess, walking peoples* and *nomadic intent*, for example, and *not-in-my-backyard* approaches to homestead management, all of which illustrate the capitalizing of resources for exploitative profit. In particular, the term *improvement* for the purpose of advocacy when justifying territorial seizure, in the sense that *we* will use the resources *better* than those who currently have *use* of them. Improvement is often a cloak by which to dispossess and displace *undesirable* elements, those presenting unwelcome race and or class attributes.

The word *improve* is based on the older French for "profit."

For improvement read *renewal*, and *nostalgia*, for Boym "the fantasies of the past, determined by the needs of the present, [that] have a direct impact on the realities of the future."

A nested term inside these lines of thought, the older Latin term, *rus in urbs*, creates illusions of *countryside*, by building a garden within a city.

inanimals: all of us on this planet who are fighting and losing the battle for clear breath. See **unanimals** (a synonym which is also an antonym).

indigenous ecopoetics foregrounds how the primary themes in native texts express the idea of interconnection and interrelatedness of humans, nature, and other species; the centrality of land and water in the conception of indigenous genealogy, identity, and community; and the importance of knowing the indigenous histories of a place. Moreover, indigenous ecopoetics shows how native writers employ ecological images, metaphors, and symbols to critique colonial and Western views of nature as an empty, separate object that exists to be exploited for profit. Last, indigenous ecopoetics reconnects people to the sacredness of the earth, honors the earth as an ancestor, protests against further environmental degradation, and insists that land (and literary representations of land) are sites of healing, belonging, resistance, and mutual care.

inhabitant: an organism that cultivates and deploys knowledge of biotic community, contributes to sustaining life processes, seeks meaningful material relations beyond ecologically irrelevant political boundaries, seeks familiarity with plants and animals, geographical specificities, and so on; if human, engages this knowledge through place-making practices toward a viable, meaningful, protected, sustainable home. Examples not limited to engineering water management systems (beaver), restoring native plant communities (Aldo Leopold), creating pollinator sanctuaries (President Obama's "Butterfly Corridor"), protecting treaty rights, tending small nests and gardens. Also, the writing of such an organism.

inter-strand, drawing on Kamau Brathwaite's "interlap," a landscape metaphor for the process of creolization in the Caribbean. A landscape poetics that gives a dynamic and three-dimensional way of thinking about habit and habitat, human and nonhuman activities and interventions—as fissured *and* fluid (more than "in the cracks" / palimpsest), brushing past, reaching through. Waves' edge procession and recession, carrying and uncovering; the connections between cargos and wrecks, sparks and dissolution. In canyons, cities, beach, and backlands: seeds displaced from one shelf to another, bearing crumbs of dirt. Sideways ramifications: new roots, new walls, new wires, new-old-new pathways. Growing/ writing over and through; speaking/living with *and* under.

inter-continents the largest spaces   not-fit the only precondition.

IOYAIENE: one can imagine a person, a Karankawa person (maybe near Laredo or maybe on the coast of el Golfo de México) some time around 1828 reciting this word and a number of others to Juan Luis Berlandier (who might be Jean-Louis Berlandier), who scribbled the words down on a paper. This paper was later sold by Berlandier's wife as part of a collection to a US American general who was occupying Matamoros in the mid-nineteenth century. We can imagine that list of words somehow traveling to London and being acquired by the British Museum at Sotheby's in 1913. We can imagine Herbert Landar finding this list of words and then reproducing it in an article in a linguistics journal in 1968. Now we can read this word being republished in 2015 on a poetry and poetics website and in the book *Ford Over* in 2016 and again in 2018 in this book. Yet in the space between 1828 and 2018 the meaning of the word has been lost. Perhaps this word (its sound, its smell, its weight, its dirt, its wetness) might be a map back to its signified, all that has been lost.

Land is a word of intimate relationship. See **akiw8gon**.

language: a living archive. A communal lung that holds and re-members all things through us. Made between our bodies, language lives everywhere. It travels and absorbs. A neural interconnectivity; the kinetic sensation is felt by all. It is composed of edges, imposes edges, but has no edges. It is a phenomenal organism, an extended nervous system that we all share. Capacious and metamorphic, infinitely adaptable, composed of and running through everything: all the meat of our bodies, this recyclable air, the earth and the universe that suspends it, all the physical spaces that contain us, and even all of the invisible, silent, or silenced spaces where language rests, waiting for us to bring our attention through sound. Language absorbs all things: silt, soil, your ear against air, each word, earth against the mouth. To make room, in language, for language, listen closely. See **repair**.

making: the act and process of creating. Making that requires mental and physical attention engages proprioception, allows the sensation of body-being-in-place. This might mean handwork—writing by hand, or manipulating objects that represent language in space (or sound) rather than in mind or onscreen. It might mean interspersing meditation or movement with writing, or practicing a craft with physical products—whittling, knitting, repair—in tandem with poetic practice. See Wendell Berry's "work that is restorative, convivial, dignified and dignifying, and pleasing" ("The Body and the Earth"). Making may disturb or exploit a place and simultaneously aid or enhance that or another place. See Bridget Elmer and Emily Larned: "Impractical Labor seeks to restore the relationship between a maker and their tools; a maker and their time; a maker and what they make" (*Impractical Labor in Service of the Speculative Arts*). Such labor may also help to restore and maintain the relationship between the maker and the places where they make.

metabolic poetics is concerned with the potential of expanded modes of reading and writing to shift the frames and scales of conventional forms of signification in order to bring into focus the often inscrutable biological and cultural writing intrinsic to the Anthropocene, especially as this is reflected in the inextricable link between the metabolic processes of human and nonhuman bodies and the global metabolism of energy and capital. We wear the energy systems that power our societies in the form of chemicals in our flesh and in the hormonal messages of the endocrine system. We house shifting communities of microbes that reflect our dependence on processed, industrialized food production. As a result of these influences, metabolic rifts have developed within human bodies and societies (obesity epidemics, income inequality) as well as within larger planetary biogeochemical cycles (increasing atmospheric carbon dioxide). How might we expand our capacity for literacy as our awareness of intertwined material-semiotic worldings grows? Attentive to diffractive methodological approaches that encompass biosemiotic, transcorporeal, and intra-active considerations, metabolic poetics includes expanded practices that conceive of poetry as an enzyme (Robert Kocik), or the hormone as a linguistics (Lisa Robertson), or diagnosis as poetics (Eleni Stecopoulos), along with other material-discursive entanglements.

metaform (adj./v.) describes the process of becoming, of physically incorporating and transforming the human and other-than-human world by way of material, embodied, and conceptual intra-action. In this process, our particular, corporeal embeddedness in the world gives rise to ideas that affect how human and other-than-human entities inhabit the world, shifting what and how the world means, generating new ideas that affect further material shifts, and so on. This concept derives from Mark Johnson's definition of mind as a continuous intra-action of human body, brain, and environment (in *The Meaning of the Body: Aesthetics of Human Understanding*). According to Johnson, metaphor plays a key role in mind's emergence. Metaphor is not a deviation from the primary or "original" meaning of a word, an understanding of metaphor that Marina Rakova calls "the standard assumption" (in *The Extent of the Literal: Metaphor, Polysemy and Theories of Concepts*), but a primary function and expression of our relational being in and with the world. *Metaform* combines *metaphor, form*, and *metamorphosis* to express the material ramifications of this logic. In line with this definition, metaphor is not a purely linguistic or conceptual figure but a linguistic expression of a very real material process; this process is "metaform."

negative corpuscuity is a fantasy field of the Anthropocene corresponding with the onset of the nuclear age after World War II, in which it was possible to imagine mass extinction enacted through human technological means and not simply as an act of gods or supernatural phenomena. The imaginative potential of *negative corpuscuity* is in conversation with Keats's "negative capability," which describes lyric possibility through the poet's self-negation, allowing for more intimate relationship between self and nature, no longer in opposition. Given that the nuclear age weaponized the exhilarating discoveries of the constituent parts of matter, *negative corpuscuity* in turn views the constituent parts of matter, which make up all our flora and fauna, as a field of "small bodies" in intimate relationship to constituent parts of the (human) self. It asks us to think of our bodies on a minute scale of energies and fields. Negative corpuscuity derives from the term *negative corpuscule* or negative body, the initial term for the electron proposed by J. J. Thomson, which was never in common usage. In other words, *negative corpuscuity* proposes to activate a different form of "atomic" imagination, one that forges small-scale connections between our material bodies and the materials of our world.

Neséíhi (pronounced neh-SAY-hih): an Arapaho verb that means "to be wild." In the Arapaho cosmology verbs go with either animate or inanimate beings (akin to the way, in Indo-European languages, words are gendered male, female, and neuter). *Neséíhi* of course is animate. It can mean to act spontaneously, to be far out, to live close to nature, to resist being meddled with, to act with notable bravery or stealth. To resist confinement furiously. For contemporary humans I'd say it means to live largely away from technological comforts or surveillance. Be skeptical of "things."

"Off the grid" is part of it—there's an edge of danger, there's more self-reliance, also stronger habits of alertness. You develop an acute sense of consequence where shouting help won't bring an ambulance.

This means that you (or a coyote, a weasel, a wolverine, a sparrow hawk) focus attention on your surroundings and study your outer and inner resources. To be *neséíhi* is not to be careless. You take care of tools, watch over weaker companions; you sing and tell stories. You also practice *níitóuuhu* (another animate verb). This means to make wild animal cries or human whistles: a mode of speech that passes directly between species.

nomensuture: a strategy of reparative nomenclature used to resist the degradation and denial of scientific fact regarding environmental conditions. Nomensuture attempts, in its insistence on clarity and truth, not only to name things as they are, but also to creatively repair and restore those things by ensuring that they are keenly seen and urgently acted on. Various strains of this linguistic suturing system have arisen in recent years, each forming in stark opposition to an instance of climate change denial or speciesism (see **dysoptics**). But its techniques are flexible and have also been wielded effectively to repair and resist other dark propagandas.

When insistently applied by organized groups, nomensutural actions can change not only public perception surrounding a sensitive environmental issue, but also affect policy, improve and repair communication across a geographic area or blighted interpersonal zone, and even rehabilitate local microclimates.

numapen: after the election, I had a dream; and in the dream, I found a word. I woke up repeating it, almost a mantra; and every day since, I've said the word to myself, trying to discover its definition. Here is the etymology as best I can construct it. Numa was the second king of Rome. He put aside Romulus's warlike ways and, to curb the violence of his people, made himself an example of humility and virtue. After his wife died, he walked through the fields every day with a nymph, who dictated to him the sacred pieties, which later he wrote down in a book. He built a temple to Jupiter whose doors were to be open when Rome was at war. During his whole reign, those doors never opened; when he died, his books were buried with him. But the etymology of *numapen* is also homonymic (*pneumapen*) and refers to spirit, breath, and, in a Homeric light, an aspect of the soul itself. The *numapen*, properly defined, is a writing tool imbued with peace, humility, breath, and soul, making possible a writing practice devoted to the same.

odontomancy: divination by teeth. To predict storms, we watch how the animals move. The chickens know before we do; we watch them pecking at their food and see them predicting a tornado that soon arrives: this is alectryomancy. Like reading tea leaves (tasseomancy) or the bones of similar chickens after a meal (osteomancy), alectryomancy attempts to divine the future from leftovers, but in contrast to those rituals, the one who moves the interpreted object is an animal. In odontomancy, the interpreted object is not consequent but potential to that animal. Under some conditions chickens can still grow teeth, ancient like flightless feathered dinosaurs. In response to environmental conditions, elephants have stopped forming tusks. To extract the full tusk-tooth, the elephant must be killed, as a third of the elongated incisor is embedded in the elephant's head. Thus the elephant-poaching industry has driven elephants near extinction. However, very rapidly in the evolutionary timeline, even rapidly in the context of punctuated equilibrium, elephants have stopped growing these teeth over the course of two or three generations. Under the right conditions toothless animals refer back to their ancient DNA. Teeth to shred, teeth to chew, teeth to bare. When they are needed. What can we predict by the presence or loss of teeth in a species?

orakinzop: *oratory* often sits in the shape of an empty throne. Why not a mystical boat shaped like the body of our vowels, our owls, head and smart tail and eyes of a bird? Truth's imagination. Its hooting. Its connectivity in relative space and time. The shape of weather. *Kin*, related to *kind* and *child* from *akin*, and see also *cynn, kunjam, kenn, kyn*: family, race, sort, rank. Then there's *kunzop*, Buddhism's "relative truth," Tibetan, which posits the notion of "dressed up." The dressed-up world is hard to work with because it is said to be empty of its own nature. It fills gaps of all kinds. *Kunzop* is an outfit, a costume, a self-existing show, a performance, an orality, "a living theater." As a performer in the relative world, you want it to be about you and things seen your way. "You could be the audience or you could be the show." We disagree. There's rampant ignorance, bigotry, misogyny, racism, and ideology that want to enforce their versions of truth. Distinction between unreasonable and reasonable logic breaks down, goes psychotic. When we meditate, we might start to realize what is known as the transparency and impermanence of time and space. (Absolute truth?) And feel akin to everyone with a broken heart, all sentience. The whole picture keeps shifting under our feet. But the earth we sit on as it rolls under our feet (impermanence!) can be harmed but won't be fooled. We can't remove the date from the White House website and make climate change go away as an "issue." India's hottest day on record: 123.8 degrees Fahrenheit in the town of Phalodi, India's hottest day on record. An *orakinzop* with broken heart, communication, and measurement.

orrido (from the Latin *horrĭdus*, a derivative of *horrēre*, "to feel horror" [first half of the fourteenth century]): a rocky throat of tremendous depth and beauty, formed by the action of water falling through caverns and down ravines, making for tumultuous passage into an isolated valley. Under modernity, a corridor from which electrification for other, more economically generative valleys can be drained.

the other: to talk about "the other" seems to predetermine violence against this other. Actually, the mere usage of the word *other* is itself a form of violence, even if it is used in a tolerant and accepting context. To acknowledge that differences exist *without* adhering or implying a whole or an identity: a skin color is merely different than another skin color, for example, or a genital is merely different than another genital. When "the other" is an impenetrable whole and not just mere differences, violence is possible: a person of color is formed by taking one—already constructed—feature and reducing a living breath to it. This is symbolic violence par excellence. An identity, final and rigid, hence an "other," also and by necessity final and rigid. Relying on the category of "mere differences," in contrast, could help establish an ontologically flat surface where few points of attack/violence can present itself.

overburden: that tear of ecosystem, or stratum of *landscape* (earth set apart by human perception, cf. *country*, from *contra*), poor in life designated as *natural resources*, or *economically exploitable substances*, such as ore bodies, coal seams, or museal artifacts of institutionally corroborated history, and enduring above the same—hence to be blasted open and trucked *away*, to some *periphery classified as equally profitless*, so that *exploitation (the action of benefiting from assets)* may commence.

ovulept: the mediation, disruption, and restructuring of ovulatory time by anthropogenic environmental factors including lungfull emissions, endocrine disruptors, hazy particulates. Also: the reshuffling of ovulatory time's various markers by anthropogenic time: thwarting, mediating, stalling, occluded, corporatized, post-Fordist, market-based approaches to temporality as a condition for subjectivity or livedness or duration. Reproduction's split into marketable commodities, egg as service, tissue as surplus, cells' liquid journeys via transnational channels of reproductive labor. Occluded from view by a small round word; no safe passage; it doesn't last or stick; it sinks. A letter written in thick dark ink. Time and the slippage of a tiny physical object, time congealed, a bleeding sunset. An incantation is repeated so is an argument meant to persuade time to bend like a sentence. As feathers are not flowers and a toxic California sunset repeats until it doesn't.

(A term meant to be deployed within discourses of reproductive time, queer futurity, and the market economy of ovulatory crisis.)

page-making: the human act of using available surfaces and environments as sites and materials in or with which to produce writing. This can be an outdoor or indoor, digital or material, actual, imagined, or conceptual activity. It expresses the ubiquity of the page as a frame of reference within or by which we cast the world around us as a vehicle for human expression. "Page-making" usually casts the human author as the primary agent in the production of writing, and therefore the "page-making" process, while the other-than-human material is cast as the page. Occasionally this dialectic is troubled or confused, particularly when attention is drawn to the other-than-human makeup of the words themselves, to the agency of the "page" or when an obstacle is encountered to frustrate the author's original intention. Very occasionally this dynamic is reversed, when the human figures as a page for other-than-human writing. "Page-making" emerges out of a long-standing process of environmental cultural processing; its troubling and reversal offer methods of eroding and transforming the dynamics of "page-making" so as to explode the stable meaning complex from which it develops. "Page-making" highlights the role that the technology, materials, and accompanying ideology of writing have had in defining our understanding of human and other-than-human agency and authorship. See also Heidegger's *The Question concerning Technology* and Tim Ingold's *Lines*.

Panamá is a faraway place. It is the crack in the egg of the world. It joins the Oceans and the Sea. It joins the hemispheres as the Bridge of the World. It is a place of many fishes and the homeland of the liminal (though it is not limited to the liminal). Panamá's population is infinite and uncountable, animate and inanimate, of every form, every color . . . with no center or origin necessarily observable. The Panamanian person is not limited to flesh, not bound by any Western or Eastern category or mode. The heart of a Panamanian is evenly distributed throughout the multiverse. Partly because of its evenly distributed nervous system, the cockroach is a Panamanian's totem insect. There is no boundary to Panamá in any of the seven directions. Panamá as spiritual state is made up of all possible valences. Because the domain and the target of the spiritual state of Panamá include everything between past time and contradiction as well as the poles of each path of dichotomy, Panamá is more closely related to the structure and the quantum nature of the qubit than to the binary structure and nature of the bit. The third space grows from everything in Panamá, even in the partisan and in the otherwise not in-between. Panamá is shaped like a snake, a supremely yogic animal. Panamá is the country of union, hence and because of its ancient indigenous yoga ("yoga" as a putting together; see also **Saloma** and **Tecumseh Republic**). It is the country of mediation, part of an ever-proliferating symbol of completion joining the hemispheres, connecting near to far.

path (after G. F. Dutton and Frank Fraser Darling):

a path should merge into the wild on either side
a path holds the foreground and assembles vision,
    just as far as the horizon
paths are interludes in-between episodes
a path is not static — it wanders past Time
a path is never straight, no matter how flat the country
trust a deer path over a human path
plan a path with broad feet & narrow eyes

pathmaking: a bridge between language and nondiscursive or preliterate hermeneutics, such as divination or the reading of animal tracks (see Carlo Ginzburg, *Clues, Myths, and the Historical Method*). Verse then (the plow's turn) as infrastructural recompense in an era that has disposed of the notion of "public works."

permeability: a porousness that insists upon the copresence of the other, of the outside, of the self as other. Insistence on a copresence, while simultaneously allowing for moments of distance, for moments to draw back, to refuse, and also to reenter. A state of compassion and vulnerability that is an opening of the self and an acknowledgment of the various systems (people, objects, animals, ecosystems, histories) that compose the self. A push against erasure, a struggle to prevent multiplicity from destroying the possibility of a whole. An insistence on the metaxy of the body and bodiless, of the ground and groundlessness, of past and present. Neither subsuming, nor digesting, nor rejecting the various components that comprise and challenge.

phylogeny: coined by Ernst Haeckel (think drawings of diatoms, shells, jellyfish, spiders, etc.), 1866, to describe the organismal lineages we all passed through; *phyla* (φυλή, tribe, stem, race, branch) + *geny* (born). Troubled by Haeckel's repugnant ideas of a hierarchy of "races." Wrest it from his hands and give it back to all the animals and plants — we all passed through roots and branches of the same tree, beginning somewhere with a few molecules combusting (as Darwin suspected, as genome data confirms). In the mid-1960s, Lynn Margulis pioneered "symbiogenesis": we came about not just through competition but through acts of symbiosis. We carry evidence of species merger in our cells, of species relation in almost every structure we daily rely on. Lobefin fishes did proto-lungs, acorn worms might have done something like a heart, amphibians did shoulders, jellyfish saw first. If we let phyla be taken over by its bedmate phylla (leaves, petals, sprouts, sheaves, sheets of paper), we clear a mute space where we are all tangled in and leafing from the same roots. (If we take it further, to its homonymic neighbor, *philo*, we fall into love.)

phytosentience: plant intelligence. The knowledge of and by ourselves as nervous branchings. Phytosentience is that awareness of intelligences that rouse at the light, are stressed or unstressed in varying temperatures and pressures, and are coded, like the Venus flytrap, to acknowledge touch. "Plant-thinking, like the thinking of our own bodies, is neither conceptual nor pictorial," writes Michael Marder. The deep consideration of the being of the plant, the cognitive-emotional-imaginative process of thinking oneself as plant, feels good. Plants' awareness — their communicative capacities, their potential to learn, their phototropism — is phytosentience. To be aware of plants' awareness is a form of phytosentience. We use phytosentience to feel into ourselves, opening consciousness in that part of us poetic percussion pleases. It's the sentience it takes to be grounded at soily root chakra while crown chakra's thousand petals open above the head. As Ronald Johnson wrote: "Linkings, inklings / around the stem & branches of the nervetree / shudder & shutterings, sensings. / SENSE sings."

place-name (after W. F. N. Nicolaisen):

a place-name is a sound-designating reality
place-names are composed of words for what a place once was
place-names color the horizon sink their roots into the past
a name is the place and its absence
place-names frame

polychronography: temporalities smeared across various stylistics in order to reveal and investigate material flows and networks perceived through the sequential process of writing and reading from an individual point of view. To overlay and to loop, to name and to elaborate, to clarify by deliberate mash-up. To name measurements of time reflexively and make awareness of multiple flows incantatory—a poetics of temporal and temporary reverie. To embed personal events within human and more-than-human temporalities. To make referents slippery, to let action in one time flow become a current in another. To use sounds as connectives across temporalities. To body time. To fracture and to reassemble as supernovas explode only to coalesce at distance into new clouds that make new stars. Polychronography requires cut-ups and attenuations, glints off hyperobjects perceived from this portion of the electromagnetic spectrum and even writing the instrumentation of access, be it a PET scan or a radio observatory. Polychronography recognizes and enacts multiple understandings of temporality, including time as a synonym for life itself and time as measurement. It can wade into deep time, the deep present, globalization's collapse of time zones, and even models of the universe that exile time.

protector: guardian, defender, one who stands for an element, a place, a sustenance, a human right, indigenous spirituality/connection/stewardship rights.

Origins: #noDAPL in the Sacred Stone Camp, Standing Rock Sioux versus DAPL.

Use: to differentiate between protest show of action and prayerful, devoted dedication to protecting clean water source(s) from highly probable contamination by the oil industry.

Use: (2016) by Sacred Stone Camp, Oceti šakowiŋ Camp, Red Warrior Camp, unilaterally by all Water Protectors, allies, and allied agencies.

protext is a species of political action that arises from acute crises, such as the recent rise of right-wing nationalism, the normalization of racism and misogyny, or accelerated environmental depredation. While protext is often linguistic in nature, it can also proceed by way of visual or cultural literacies, or other, extraliterary forms of signification. Protext can issue from the expressive possibilities of new media—the writing of computer code (to cite but one example) can be a form of protext. While certainly political, protext is not programmatic, and its orientation is responsive rather than reactionary: the prefix *pro-* suggests affirmation, a viewpoint oriented "forward, to or toward the front, from a position in the rear, out, into a public position" (*Oxford English Dictionary*). Because protext is often a highly localized phenomenon, its performance is frequently inflected with anxieties about its own efficacy and whether its energies are communicable.

radical empathy: to be radical is to be extreme, to hold intense conviction, to come out of a rooted place and, in an atomic sense, to behave as a unit. What would it mean to deploy empathy in such a way?

Radical Indigenous Queer Feminist: a person that lives on the intersections of radical thought and whose politics and daily rituals are rooted in survival or acts of survivance while reclaiming and empowering themselves and their communities through their indigenous culture, ceremony, and traditional practices. This person is just as powerful and intelligent with or without having been institutionalized by the colonizers who have corrupted the harmony human beings have nurtured alongside the land, water, sky, animals, and plant life since time immemorial. In acknowledging the term *Radical Indigenous Queer Feminist*, the individual is aware of the power of reclaiming Western/English theoretical terms as a means to critique those spaces in order to engage in discussion about histories that have been erased or altered through genocide, forced assimilation, and incalculable acts of colonial violence. The histories include, but of course could never be limited to, matrilineal/matriarchal societies and leadership, reverence toward nonbinary/multigender societies, nontoxic/Western forms of masculinity that function outside the praxis of patriarchy, and various forms of sexual orientation that aren't constrained by Western constructs of heterosexuality or homosexuality.

reassociated: the body knows what the voice cannot. To return to the body when it has been taken from you, build a body safer than your own that you can fit inside. This might be a cocoon of moss and loam, woven in the loose shape of you. It could be a box of water, within which you can float until you are ready to emerge as if for the very first time. Or a book built of plaited sentences that rewrite a life safer than your own. See **bodied**.

reciproesis is from the words *reciprocity* (a balanced giving and taking of equals) and *poesis* (making or doing). *Reciproesis* is our doing in response to *listening*. *Reciproesis* arises from the understanding that all making, all doing, is done in reciprocity with the **Land**. *Reciproesis* grows from the knowledge that we are persons among other persons, that we live in gratitude for the gifts given freely—for example, the water that gives itself to us, the green plants that make food and oxygen from sunlight and freely give it to us all—that our making must be a giving back informed by our respectful *listening*, our gratitude, and our willing and conscious participation in **akiw8gon**. I believe that the indigenous knowledge contained in these words is crucial in creating a paradigm change in Western understanding that will help us choose the green road rather than the road of cinders. See **akiw8gon**, *Land.*

reconstructive cladistics: the reparatory capacity to perceive, in the mind's mirror, traces of the cephalon, pygidium, glabella, and so on, of one's relatives in self, in otherness; and the flowering effects of this capacity on the quality of immediate somatic experience.

recovery: to take cover and protect, dissemble, tear down, and replace. *Recovery*: from Old French "expressing intensive force""—force like a weed, seeded in the crack and grown. A vine that tears down walls and reclaims. Conceal. To make crumble. To know something about who and what we are. To be agent by which we repair; to live as immune system; to resemble a weed's capacity for self-regeneration.

relaxation time has to do with how extinction processes occur. When a species is under pressure, their survival might continue for a lengthy duration before they succumb to total annihilation. This process of time delay is called *relaxation time* (and the phenomenon is also known as *extinction debt*). This time-based understanding of collective death relates intimately to the Anthropocene—a period in which we are currently undergoing a massive loss of biodiversity. What are the threshold conditions for human animals, other animals, and all other coproducers of life on earth? How can a future be imagined when there is a violent loss of biocultural diversity? More than a hundred species go extinct on a daily basis, yet this event takes place unregistered for most human animals. *Relaxation time* speaks to the way we as human animals perceive our relationship to other animals and the ecosystem. We hardly notice animals (ourselves and others) as well as flora relaxing out of existence.

repair: begin with what you have. Here, a clutch of syllables tied with blue string—carnation, elderflower, gardenia, thyme, and thistle. A white candle. A ring of hair. Ink. Let it warp. To gather all absences through a door in the tongue. Silence to sound to skin, to restore all things. See **language**.

repoise: Let's call it the inner-eruptive tense (not future, not present, not past) emerging from *repose*. To *repoise* is to *not deny* or avoid the poison of an all-consuming-and-deadening event, be it a personal, local, political, or global poison. To repoise is to act *within* what I have been, and am, and may become. To find in the midst of a poison's numbness an *i* hiding inside the deadness of repose, an *i* that is a tincture made of the poison, a little *i* right there, in the midst of the numbness, an *i* born of the disruption, brought awake, despite the vortex of loss surrounding me, an *i* that makes *poise* possible, shocking as that may feel. Repoising reaches back, down, and forward at once, edgy, itchy with interest, and a little dangerous, a bridge-tense moving fast, but one that is not the "bridge" of past-perfect or present-perfect or future-perfect. The little *i* in repoise makes it a tense that is never perfected, never complete.

resistance: to be rooted and unruly. To be integrated into local circumstance so to dismantle monoliths. To challenge monolithic orders and defy language itself, to defy the ways of the castle. To deeply see is to seek the roots upward, downward, and sideways. To see which processes monoliths serve. To counter forgetting and root, to expand and recognize stories beyond the monolith. Working with both roots and methods of dispersal. To seek outside usual patterns of perception by seeing the familiar in its multiple possibilities. To make against the production of unseeing.

ruins: not marble, nor gilded monuments, and so on (see Shakespeare), but abandoned strip malls, condemned housing projects, empty storefronts, half-constructed corporate headquarters ("that rise into *ruin*" — Robert Smithson), and foreclosed homes.

The United States has more *ruins* than any developed country (Mike Davis). They constitute the most consistent product of capitalism's voracious and capricious appetite, our monuments, more Rushmore than Rushmore.

Freud likened the mind to a city built over the *ruins* of a hundred ancient cities and believed we must uncover the ruts and roads, parapets and archways, over which the self is made.

Everything tends toward its end (ref. mortality or entropy). We tear down, we level, we wire the old casino with explosives. In a crash of rubble, cloud of particle, "all that is solid melts into air" (Karl Marx). But for a moment or month, however long we let our *ruins* stand, we might look to weeds growing in parking lots, pull back plywood shutters, and witness in them a rewiring, a reworking, a *poiesis*, a release from form.

Saloma: an entity-to-entity intensive communication, poetizing, or philosophizing based on the ancient Saloma Panameña practice (e.g., https://youtu.be/fzCdy9PfonE). Can happen internally or externally. A qubit-yogic practice. Also potentially closely related to complementary nature (e.g., Kelso and Engstrøm, *The Complementary Nature*). Can serve as a basis for coevolvement and intersubjectivity with other life-forms and/or machines. A healing poetics, philosophy, spirituality. A kind of vocal and proprioceptive yoga ("yoga" as a putting together) occurring on all possible levels and in all possible arrangements across the valley. Radical faciality. The basis and ground of interface. See **Panamá, Tecumseh Republic**.

sanctuary: a bounded space, without border. Where I am immune from gods and masters, without need of defense. Where I am inalienable. This point in time. Impassable. No birth or death allowed, only the living or dead. A place held in prayer, between heart and asphalt. Shellmound beneath the parking lot. Shining island. Church without priest or icon, only acoustic stone. Our city, ecumenical—belonging to all inhabitants of earth. The once and future university.

scalar: Isn't earth connected to sun with an intimacy distinct from the speed of light? There must be a process connecting one end of Andromeda to the other in nonlocal time by which the galactic entity operates, that is, simultaneously. We see that star-clusters near the center spin more slowly than those on the outer edge of the whirlpool. She spins, and all her stars spin with her. All connect by a force without inertia, without size or direction, that's invisible if viewed so slowly as the speed of light.

sci-animism: from the Latin *scire*, "to know," and *anima*, "life," "breath," "soul." The belief that science is a path to feeling the soulfulness of rocks and stars, plants and animals, air and sea. Not an embrace of pseudoscience or alternative facts, sci-animism argues for embracing an evidence-based love of human embeddedness in the unfolding beauty of the material world, a love that calls forth human care and intelligence. Sci-animism holds that scientific thought and animistic identification team up in the Anthropocene to guide the moral sense toward right action for a just and sustainable future (q.v. Robin Kimmerer, "Learning the Language of Animacy"). To *sci-animize* is to engage in theorizing or speculating about sci-animism; to *sci-animate* is to breathe the life of art into scientific data; to conduct field research, informed by science, that gives rise to new artistic forms. See, for example, composer DJ Spooky's (aka Paul Miller) symphonic remix "Heart of a Forest," composed during four seasonal visits to the Andrews Experimental Forest in Oregon.

shadow: Even if I'm angry the cedar was cut down, part of restoring balance is my response. New ecology, collective mind, calls for expressions of growth. When a wood lily blooms, a chord sounds. I feel tremendous energy flow from beautiful earth, for the quantum is diaphanous, not dialectic, and permeated by starlight. Time, transformation, unifies. My anger at destroyed land provides a structure that's appropriate, so I also feel peace—two emotions, side by side, natural shadow. There's still a world of contrast, but in color, not black-and-white, and in change.

shelter (noun): "I really cannot fathom visiting Hawaii again. The homeless, stench of homeless and rampant crime from . . . gangs have totally turned me off to this once beautiful [place]." "The purpose of this ordinance is to prohibit, subject to exceptions, persons from sitting or lying on city sidewalks in the Waikiki district [since expanded]." "The encampments have grown to a point where they're no longer manageable. It's really a last resort at this point for us to be able to try and manage the area . . . a new stored property law will allow city officials to seize property on public sidewalks. [Mayor] Caldwell has called this tactic a form of 'compassionate disruption' (Councilman Joey Manahan). "When people are moved and they are uncomfortable, they make different choices" (Connie Mitchell, executive director of the Institute for Human Services). "Something which affords a refuge from danger, attack, pursuit, or observation; a place of safety." "Serving as a sanctuary in ancient times for defeated warriors, noncombatants, and those who violated the kapu (sacred laws), the Pu'uhonua o Hōnaunau remains a most sacred place to those who step foot on its grounds." "Today, you may visit Pu'uhonua o Hōnaunau National Historical Park, and still feel the spirit of peace and forgiveness that continues to surround and bless this special place." "The Pope Francis Laundry— opened by the Pope himself—is a place where homeless people and others struggling with extreme poverty can wash and dry a load of laundry for free." "We can find no social or moral justification, no justification whatsoever, for lack of housing" (Pope Francis).

skirt: to lift up and away, to shirk, to walk outside or around a zone of responsibility or an imagined periphery of complicity. This describes the casual and everyday practice of imagining oneself as belonging to the outskirt, edge, or perimeter of an ecological disaster, both morally and physically. As observed in the act of kith lifting their saris and under-petticoats to walk around, beyond, past, or attempting to otherwise physically transcend symptoms of ecological disasters in urban contexts—oil seepage into ground-gutters, toxic wells, garbage mounds, human waste tributaries—in order to perform a moral transcendence of responsibility and codependence on urbanization, underfunding of municipal sanitation, informal or gray economies, and complicity with hazardous and substandard housing. As an everyday practice, skirting attempts to construct a cognitive map (see Fredric Jameson) in order to perceptually and imaginatively neuter one's own social alienation from the urban "barrage of immediacy," where the cause and effect of environmental policy, like a diesel-fueled high-octane ouroboros, shit and eat the simultaneous fragmentation and homogenization of urban space. Skirting is a daily practice—lifting yards of chiffon, cotton, silk, and rayon blends away from organic and man-made waste— that underpins (but does not underwrite) a "system of operational combination" (Michel de Certeau) composing a culture of consumption. It pulls back, folds away, lifts up, and partitions any zone of contact between the disaster and the self. See **unskirt**.

slow violence: from Rob Nixon: "A violence that occurs gradually and out of sight, a violence of delayed destruction that is dispersed across time and space, an attritional violence that is typically not viewed as violence at all" (*Slow Violence and the Environmentalism of the Poor*). What forms of slow violence am I participating in? Name them. What can I do to meaningfully reduce that participation, to reverse that violence, or parts of it? Nixon: "A major challenge is representational: how to devise arresting stories, images, and symbols adequate to the pervasive but elusive violence of delayed effects." Work at this with lyric, with narrative, with other forms.

solastalgia: a "psychoterratic" or earth-related mental health condition, solastalgia is psychic or existential distress caused by environmental change. Australian environmental philosopher Glenn Albrecht coined the term after studies on long-term drought and mining activity revealed there was no word to describe the unhappiness of people whose landscapes were being transformed by forces beyond their control. Solastalgia—Latin *sōlācium*, *sōlātium*, the stem of *sōlārī*, "to comfort, console," and *algia*, "pain"—thus emerged to describe this distinctive kind of homesickness. Indigenous inhabitants of Australia's Hunter Valley experience solastalgia relative to large-scale open-cut coal-mining impacts and will travel hundreds of extra kilometers to avoid looking at what has been done to their home.

south borderland: two nations or two ideologies abut. Theoretically the walls are omnipresent, but blurry and evanescent. The borderland is a collision of two ontogenies, though not demarcated. The difference is apparent in the people on either side, on their houses and the origin of their colonizer and that colonizer's lasting impression in the landscape. Inside the borderland are the furies and the disruptions. Violence is a fog here. History is effaced by populist amnesia, so in theory, one side is still a fresh occupation to the displaced on either side. The border is the acute mirror to our hungers.

sus-ten-ance: *sustento* refers to food, to livelihood, something that provides nourishment or support. It's growth but it's also a hold. The bounce of earth underneath my feet. But this is a give-and-take. We can't be supported solely by a hollow tree; it bends, then breaks.

Tecumseh Republic: among other things . . . a postcolonial, postrace, post–united states, postbinary, postcomputer, postcapital, posthuman/newly human, postoppression, post-Indian societal ontology respectful of and led by traditional holistic indigenous values. Named after the Shawnee leader Tecumseh (b. 1768–d. October 5, 1813), who in the early nineteenth century almost succeeded in uniting an Indian nation in victory against the largely mass-murdering and racist United States. Citizens of the Tecumseh Republic are known as Tecs and have absorbed and transcended all technologies previous to the endpoint of empire. The Tecumseh Republic is reachable through el Cerro Sonsonate and other spiritual highpoints in Panamá. In this way, Panamá is the Tecumseh Republic's only entrance and its only exit. No Tec is mediated by the screen, and all emphasize both internal and external face to face communication. The Tecumseh Republic is borderless and permeates all worlds on some level. See **Panamá**, **Saloma**.

temenos: from the Greek *tem-* / to mark / to **cut** / to **precinct** / to sanctuary / land designated to a king or dedicated to a god, a sanctuary, a holy grove or precinct, such as the Acropolis of Athens.
    —a **receptacle of divinity**—a **locality**—a cup—
    —a *walking grove of sacred trees*—a threshold—

:: of mind :: of transmission communion :: of **magic** ::
:: of prophecy :: of dream :: of mtn forest river ocean ::
:: of ten thousand directions ::
& all sound **soundings** mystic universe thought speech proces-
sion *to light and then return.*

terraqué: combines *terra* (earth) and *aqua* (water) to convey the
variable existence(s) between the two. I first came across the term
while translating Michèle Métail's long poem *Les horizons du sol*
(*Earth's Horizons*):

HAUTS-FONDS SI SUBMERSIBLES QUE MASQUE DEPUIS LE
SOIR L'AGITATION ENCLAVÉE DANS UN MONDE TERRAQUÉ

In the global context of troubled waters—drought, sea-level rise,
megastorms—the word echoed and continued to sound. I wanted
to keep the sense of an agitated world caught between two ele-
ments, the harshness of the *q* extending into unresolvable tension.

SUBMERGED SHOALS THAT DURING THE NIGHT MASK THE
ANXIETY OF A WORLD HELD BETWEEN EARTH AND WATER

Instead, I chose the *x* of anxiety: *X* for the tremble of change.

terrotic: to be aroused—especially to action, conservation, rewil-
ding, writing and/or revolution—by (or in) ecology, physical ge-
ography, and/or nonhuman environments. Relating to the capacity
of the earth to awaken sexual desire or excitement [in part for har-
nessing into alternate ways of living and being on the planet]. To
desire, want, or have sexual appetites in relation to planetary forces
and their preservation. An act of humans bringing or coming to-
gether with the ecological nonhuman.

t/here: the manifold is present in the singular. Walking through the cemetery in late winter, snowdrops flower haphazardly among trees and fallen monuments across a hillside, rain dappling my skin. The dead are here, too, and not. Dogs walk, sniff, defecate, race. "Mother" and "Father" writ on stone: names from Dutch, French, German, English, Greek, Italian, Islamic diasporas. I, too, might rest here, sooner, later. Under the earth. The drumlins across which we walk, spoil dropped by retreating glaciers, scribe a deeper time frame. While the weather has borrowed the wet from Lake Ontario, the snowdrops originate in the Pyrenees, Caucasus, Iran, the Aegean. For a thousand years, the Onondaga people here dwelt, their homeland since reduced to 7,300 acres southeast of Syracuse. Lake Onondaga, birthplace of the Haudenosaunee, bears the freight of two hundred years of city sewage, commercial salt production, and heavy industry; an EPA Superfund site, though rehabilitated, remains one of the nation's most polluted lakes. In the seams of my shoes, traces of south Louisiana mud adheres. Here and there, now and then. All at once. All. At. Once. Hold that, be *t/here*.

thereoir: the markings that make a city legible; the conversation between the languages of infrastructure (markings on roads and sidewalks made by utility workers) and graffiti (markings on walls and trestles and tunnels), speech & reading, art & crime, necessary & nuisance, renovation & revolution: between pigeons as fancy & menace.

Thereoir is how some civic language is sanctioned vandalism: necessary (marking existing utilities or where new ones should go, where something is to be built or unbuilt) & some, misdemeanor (un-asked-for, without permission). It's a matter of who makes language and where, who makes signs & do those signs say progress or decay.

Thereoir is identification & anonymity, claiming territory, concealing authors.

Thereoir is resistance, encoding, writing inside-languages outwardly, communicating ambiguity.

Thereoir is the character & climate of cities, the features of a landscape we see and, in seeing them, read and make meaning.

torpor might describe the rest state required of an activist. An activist might enter a state of torpor so that she can continue to thrive despite the onset of particularly difficult weather and reduced resources. After a period of torpor, the activist may be extraordinarily hungry and aggressive, better prepared for a busy and demanding season of long days and nights. In her torpor state, an activist maintains her base convictions, but she will significantly slow her mental and physical activities. In this way, she will be able to protect her overall longevity. Even from a state of torpor, the activist can wake up rapidly and thoroughly if necessary. Torpor does not last long relative to the activist's fully alert periods, though for the health of the activist, torpor may recur on something akin to an annual basis.

unanimals: to replace *animals*; to recognize that the original meaning of *animals* simply denotes breathing and is not a separation/distinction between a false human/other species binary, nor an insult to our mammalian and evolutionary nature, for example, "What are you, an animal?" Yes, you are. We are. We humans are animals, and our animalnesses could—if we let it—unite and connect us to other sentient beings of our planet. But, with human development, that vital truth has gone extinct (like so many animal species). *Unanimals* reminds us that we ought to make a collective effort toward the unified and diverse needs and benefit of all of us who take breath. See **inanimals**.

unpersonism: wherein the poetic subject is a site of total permeability, of radical interconnection with the human and nonhuman living world. Not so much a negation as a dilation of Frank O'Hara's "Personism"—which famously proposes an eros of poetic abstraction that evokes "overtones of love without destroying love's life-giving vulgarity . . . while preventing love from distracting into feeling about the person." Unpersonism proposes a more inclusive embrace, an eros that extends from the intraspecies to the cross-species to the planetary, with "all life-giving vulgarity" intact.

Unpersonism can be poetically manifested by many means, including a probing of one's position in time and space, in which the individual dissolves into the gene pool, the species into the ecosystem, and the ecosystem into a continuum of changing relationships and dependencies. At its most extreme, unpersonism may extend out to the universe, where it attains a state of cosmic anonymity, a form of the ultimate communal. At another extreme, it conjures an image of a rock formation in which human fossil remains lie intermingled with evidence of mass plant and animal extinctions. It is this apparition of future ruin that compels the backward-facing angel of history to turn around and face her destiny as the angel of the Anthropocene.

unskirt: to touch the disaster. To touch, not with the vulnerable body: the warm, bony ankle dampened by sewage; the full, dark calves splashed by the well water swirling with mercury; the muscles atrophying with government-sanctioned toxicity; the heaving sorrow and nausea of entire towns. But to touch the disaster as a body politic by wrapping ourselves together in the yards of a constitutional right to protect what is ours—our bodies, our wells. See **skirt**.

use without using: to practice "use" nonexploitatively. Which is to say, to use not just toward "renewal" (recycling, remediation) or "sustainability" (the preservation of natural resources under capitalism) but with a more radical sense of ecology guided by nonexploitative relation in thought and practice. Whereas *using* in this context implies "using up" (exhausting, destroying), *use* suggests taking up something with (a) future (user) in mind. Use also implies mindfulness of that which is being used (as a respected object or subject of mutual recognition). Use without using is an ethical-political practice that is anticapitalist, antimisogynist, antiracist, and anticolonial because it perceives these categories as integral to the imminence (and immanence) of ecological catastrophe. One could do worse than to look to indigenous nations/groups for models of *use without using* in practice, since such groups see land use as coextensive with correct political, economic, and legal practices (health, justice, governance, kinship, aesthetics). One could also do worse than to look to those who have been denied much by the currently dominant modes of political and economic life (capitalism, neoliberalism, settler-colonialism) because, by necessity, they have innovated on the meanings of *use without using* in practice. What, for instance, are the forms of *use without using* that emerge through "zones of non-being"—Frantz Fanon's phrase for the desert-like (sociopolitical, economic, and legal) climates in which colonized and dominated subjects persist?

viral avatar: At the jubilant vertex of the most mathematically serene viral coding, we achieve viral avatar, the host in whose farthest cell a particular virus has most plentifully inscribed its formula. While multiple viruses abide contentedly in a given, begotten biome, there are chronospheric fields in which a discreet virus might insert its name so repeatedly as to become synonymous with host. This virus attains its crown, its mantle, its avatar form. As travels the host through the world, so travels the virus, spelled aloft. The human host generally refers to union as love, but shuns viral eros. We cannot explain the pain this engenders. The animal host regards union as survival, but similarly shuns viral bios. The plant host knows union to be vibration, but would rather sever from its root than transcend to viral rhizome. The fungal host recedes. The bacterial host chars its garment. Our hosts find only the other to be toxic. They wish to make a pure sound for a pure ear in its clean colony alone. They crave no vibration other than cradle. The oyster mushroom, the dysentery bacillus, the bat, the willow, the saint, the limbic other. We cannot explain the pain this engenders, and even less reject the union.

vivitocracy: a social mind-set built on the idea that all life deserves *equally* to exist. No discernible characteristics enable a hierarchy of value to subsist among life-forms of any kind in such communities. In a vivitocracy, "meaningful expressions of care," to quote Fred Rogers, are rampant and undeniable.

Small vivitocracies have been seen throughout history in times of immediate crisis and are destined to proliferate in the present day. After Hurricane Katrina, the *Atlantic* published "Finding Solidarity in Disaster," an article about vivitocracies that formed; according to its author, Jacob Remes, "disasters serve as reminders that everyone is dependent on their friends and neighbors, and that those relationships need not be mediated by the state. Indeed, they are often better left unstructured by the state."

Vivitocracies arise on their own out of mutual respect, concern, and need. The current global environmental crisis requires vivitocracies in order for the planet as we know it to survive.

walking: movement through an environment whether sinuous or along a rational transect that opens space up to time and embeds time in space. The mode of transport scaled to the human body. The nondirected activity that introduces us to our neighbors, with mutual opportunities for eye contact, smell, sound, communication. An extension of writing, on foot and in the air. An ecopoetics beyond the "house" of *oikos*, walking, writing, and/or drawing are the beginning of (human) ecology; otherwise, we are just dealing with one another's needs from the outside, with little opportunity for noncoercive exchanges within a commons. Walking makes a line, tracing the irreversible, time-bound condition of the human metabolism (cf. Richard Long). Like a transect or (famously) Thoreau's railroad cutting, walking reveals at the same time that it encloses.

washland refers to the specific laundering (as with money) of a city park located between the downtown business district and an impoverished community undergoing gentrification in Cincinnati, Ohio. *Washland* also refers to any cleansing (e.g., by oil—see Standing Rock, merely the most recent example of neocolonial betrayal of treaties between conqueror and conquered) of a land, a cleansing of its biological, geological, and/or marine forms of life in order to extract its nonliving resources. The United States of America is merely one country that can also be called *washland*, but to the extent this cleansing—primarily ethnic—was never complete (Native Americans were not driven to extinction), "we" have a moral imperative to resist the totalization of bio-geo-ethno-cleansing however much such erasures have found revived inspiration in the imminent future.

watershed: At the confluence of two rivers, the Schuylkill and the Delaware, William Penn settled his city in 1682. Built on the southeastern edge of fertile Pennsylvania piedmont, Philadelphia tilts; its creeks and stormwater drain into the Delaware's great basin. From landscaped lawns to the Wissahickon to the Schuylkill, from city streets to the Tacony to the Delaware—all the water that falls and runs works its way, if it can, south, to the Atlantic. Everything the water touches leaves traces that travel with it: lead, chromium-6, Roundup, PFAS, mercury, benzene, sulfuric acid. Plastics and microplastics. Hormones, antidepressants, countless pharmaceuticals. Because the rivers flow through our bodies, too: raw river water, once treated and drinkable, enters us and exits as urine and other fluids that flow back into the Delaware after they too have been treated. The water holds on to everything treatment doesn't remove. Though land, city, bodies all shed water, water, that universal solvent, can't shed its own memory, can't help but tell us of all it has touched.

way-dwelling:
- length of time spent in a single spot, say, when transfixed by the first spring call of a cuckoo
- enthralled
- cherry blossoms may be enjoyed for a week
- deep compassion for the place in the moment
- the unfamiliar foothold of immediacy
- waves are sea's way-dwelling
- a second of low winter sun illuminating butterbur bud-nubs
- the ephemeral is a matter of timescale
- the cry of the buzzard is one with the ear
- an involuntary surrender to place and time

weave watching: residing in the flow of the visual with another being's resonating body.

At the Point Reyes lighthouse, a gray whale weaves in and out of the surf in a glistening patch of the Pacific. What is it for the whale to come in and out of our sight, to see the whale's intelligence and desire weave through water and air, to understand a negotiation of needs and desires? A snack, then a spout. Why is the feeling medicinal to watch a fluid body surfacing and submerging? A rock or plant or animal, luxuriating in its form, weaves through mediums. Does the whale feel being seen?

Jean-Luc Nancy distinguishes the timeliness of sensing: *The visual persists until its disappearance; the sonorous appears and fades away into its permanence.* But the visual can dive and also resurface. This resurfacing is the wild, hopeful, vulnerable, and unexpected of the unknown. It is an anticipatory consciousness. Nothing in sight is stable. Everyone's fluidity's a multispecies event. When we keep our form in sight, sight weaves us, and our intelligence can be carried within it.

witness: witnessing involves an idea of significance equivalent to truth. "Earth from deep space looks blue and alive, they said . . . I heard words, but the sound carried different meaning to my body . . . . 'Use these new words, enhanced by your imagining, to allow dimensions to emerge,' they said." Care is required for witness to resonate energetically with listener, however nonchalant I appear. The more compassion one has for nonnormal experiences of others, the sooner mass consciousness will shift toward the stars. To him, this means shifting the ethical structure of communicating a narrative. "I think of myself in a service capacity."

woveness: be-cause we, worlds, words are "of green stuff woven," seeded, fleeting, tendrilled, tendreled, us, this flux we freeze-frame. Our sensing—saying—severs or sutures. Be-cause language lives between breath and flesh, it can bind back (ligature, religion) inner/

outer, past (root)/future (rot, seed), thought-map/felt-ground underfoot. Voices: visceral, animal; tech and text. Context: the world is woven (too close to see). Poetics as weaving, seeing the seams, feeling a way along the threads, the web. Learning how we are made as we make. Cicada-call, cellphone, sound through skin this August night.

"SOMEWHERE INBETWEEN"

Speaking-Through Contiguity

A glowing eel in the darkness—anguish.
He clacks the beads, how to live, where to go.
Arthur Sze | "Strike-Slip"

"Life is not just networked; it *is* network,"[1] biologist David George Haskell observes, yet where in that network does the human fit? Decoder? Recoder? Master? Our species has a long, troubled history with the illusion of mastery. The spiraling causes and consequences of ecological crisis—climate change, rising sea levels, toxic landfills, poisoned water and neighborhoods, collapsing fisheries, destroyed communities—lies within a lie, or a rather, a conceit: a false dichotomy separating humankind from all other constituent elements of the living world. *Human* and *Nature*, distinct and isolate, resonate in polar opposition, leaving humankind unresponsive to our complexly interpenetrated condition: imaging ourselves cut off while deep *in the midst.*

Timothy Morton, in *Ecology without Nature*, reframes the human/other-than-human relation as "drastically collective," to emphasize the environment as a site of political imperative: "All kinds of beings, from toxic waste to sea snails, are clamoring for our scientific, political, and artistic attention, and have become part of political life."[2] Escape from this truth lies through no doorway, no slippery construct of language or argument: "we" *are* "it," inextricable from our circumstances. The point on which all else turns: within this "drastically collective" condition, how, then, as Arthur Sze asks, live? Indeed, how *write*?

Bound up in rhetorics of power, misunderstanding, and misinformation ("alternative facts," climate change denial, the profit motive's corrupting influence), language is the material of contracts, legislation, treaties, judgments, and policy, for good or ill, as well as the primary means by which writers work. Perhaps the most urgent demand on our language right now is to afford a requisite shift of understanding and action: reframing/imagining ways of seeing, inhabiting, and expressing our relation to energy, mobility, (re)production, and community. Morton, in substituting *ecological writing* for "ecomimesis"—more colloquially termed "nature writing"—articulates a critical distinction. Ecomimesis holds that "nature" might be captured on the page through description and ambience without redress to the conceptual underpinnings of the idea of "nature" itself, the reproduction of which turns on the perception that the human species is separate from nature. Ecological writing, by contrast, situates the writer *within*: contiguous, interpenetrated, vulnerable. One salutary movement in that direction, drawing on the heterogeneous, multilayered environment in which language currently operates, are the AltEPA, AltNASA, and other Twitter handles and feeds adopted in response to Trump administration efforts to censor climate science on national websites. When language slides sideways through the radically collective and interpenetrated internet, space is held open for the formerly silenced: a social, political, activist language-practice of resistance. These activists assert an ecological imperative, inspiring writers to engage in similar acts of language/political resistance. Indeed, the environmental peril of the Anthropocene demands that writers act ecologically, directly engaging with the histories, traditions, and foundational beliefs to which we are heirs, not mere cataloguers of beauty or loss.

In order to pursue a new practice of language, consider some of the bases for our current condition, first and foremost the exhausted trope "Nature." An inheritance of Romanticism, "Nature" emerged within a critical response to the aftermath of the Industrial Revolution, the closing of the commons and the pitting of the capital class against the laborer class. We are still entangled in the climactic convulsion of this crisis. Through responses both grief-filled and celebratory of what once was, the Romantics' idealized notion of the other-than-human detaches humanity from the contiguous relations and systems that make human life possible. Wordsworth's iconic poem *The Prelude* centers on this disjunction, the poet celebrating a *return* to nature "With a heart / Joyous, nor scared at its own liberty" at "shak[ing] off / *That burthen of my own unnatural self.*"[3] Burdensome, indeed, the belief that we are unnatural, and that we might only achieve a quasi-"natural" state within a pastoral Eden. Within this paradigm, "human nature" is not "nature," but an exceptional condition, a disturbed order cut off from its source—a translation of the Judeo-Christian parable of the fall from grace. Romanticism figures Nature as refuge, site of rest and renewal from the "unnatural" conditions of urban life. Paradoxically, this pastoral construction of "nature" diminishes the other-than-human—that is, *everything else*—to a "picture postcard" or catalogue of resources managed/leveraged/profited from, and this scenario leads to two possible outcomes. We can see humankind as "tourist" or interloper, "bad guy" up to no good, "pestilence" corrupting "harmony;" such reductive notions leave room for little more than remorse, guilt, and a pervading sense of failure. In a world of 7.5 billion people, shame and sorrow will not suffice. Or, adopting the biblical notion of human dominion over "the rest of creation," we can believe that humankind might somehow fully "master" the manifold, interconnected biological, (geo)chemical, and atmospheric systems within which we are embedded and on which we depend. Two faces of a single coin—an idealist, quasi-primitivistic aesthetics of Nature and violent dominion over that Nature, the expression and justification for humankind's alienation—form the ground of our being.

This sequestration of our species from all else has not only driven environmental destruction; ironically, it has also plagued the environmental movement, which as often as not has sought, understandably, to protect, via *isolation,* the natural from the human, even in face of the radical consequences of our presence inescapably active everywhere. There is *no safe distance,* an understanding essential to transforming our mind-set and behavior. Absurdly numerous, potent, and consequential, the human species is a keystone species of the so-called "natural" world. Human actions are not *un*natural, nor are they unalterable or preordained, let alone necessarily beneficial. Our cities, our means of transport, our technologies are not less natural than the sticks by which chimpanzees fish for ants, the lodges constructed by beavers, or the tunnels and dens of meerkats. This privileging via isolation of humanity from all else has formidable consequences, and not merely in the assumed "right" to extract, use, build on, waste. Consider the faith placed in technological fixes to solve the consequences of human action: the idea that levees built to contain the Mississippi will have no ill effects on the stability of the coast and all its human and other-than-human communities, including the vast and fertile fisheries on which the United States depends. Or that an old-growth forest may be clear-cut or replaced by a pine plantation without any loss of biodiversity or soil health, and without jeopardizing the stability of the hillside below which a rural "paradise" has sprung up. The segregation of humanity from nature, whether as "pestilence" or "master," strands us within the artifice of a catastrophic conceptual error, blind to the very complexity "Nature" is meant to denote. Morton sketches the consequences of this ill-fated construct in *Hyperobjects: Philosophy and Ecology at the End of the World*, unpacking the import of the term *environment*, a word, tellingly, derived from the French *environ*, meaning that which surrounds or the conditions in which one lives.

> The word *environment* still haunts us because in a society that took
> care of its surroundings in a more comprehensive sense, our idea
> of environment would have withered away. . . . Society would be so
> involved in taking care of "it" that it would no longer be a case of some
> "thing" that surrounds us, that environs and differs from us. Humans
> may yet return to the "thing" its older sense of *meeting place*. In a
> society that acknowledged that we were always already involved in our
> world, there would be no need to point it out.[4]

As noted earlier, equally problematic as and an extension of the reification of "Nature" is the long tradition of "nature writing." Morton emphasizes how nature writing, which relies on ecomimesis and ambience in attempting to blur the boundary between inner and outer, subject and object, human and other-than-human through simulation,[5] remains at a distance, evoking only an "echo" of what was known or experienced by the subject, themselves always outside that which is experienced—objectified "nature"—copying down the remembered experience from the reverie of the writing desk. Leaving dualism firmly intact, fundamentally reliant on the distance between inner and outer, nature writing brings us no closer to complex interpenetration. "Whether we think of nature as an environment, or as other beings (animals, plants, and so on), it keeps collapsing either into subjectivity or into objectivity. It is very hard, perhaps impossible, to keep nature just where it appears—somewhere inbetween."[6] Yet critically, "somewhere inbetween" remains the only condition available to us, our way forward out of our self-engineered disaster: *how obtain that inbetween place?*

Consider again Haskell's networks, "places where that tension between conflict and cooperation gets played out," resolution enacted through the transfer of information in multiple dimensions or directions, moving from the individual from isolation to immersion in dialogue, conversation, history, toward "symbiosis and cooperation."[7] When we dwell on individual experience and awareness, we lose track of the rich connectivity that characterizes all life from the interaction of cyanobacteria, minerals, water, and light in the biochemical accretionary structure of stromatolites to the dynamic flow patterns and cross-currents of a crowded city street, its sidewalks and denizens. Indeed, each distinct network is enmeshed in all the others, behaviors and responses recalibrating within surrounding activity, always in flux. The sustainability of life-as-we-know-it demands that humans focus their attention away from one self, one community, one species, outward into the vast net of being. In so doing, we return to relationship: "If we think of the world as fundamentally relational, the question is not how we block things but how we live within those relationships."[8]

Just as *human* has been isolated in its privileged position outside "Nature," so too hierarchies of worth within the classification "human" have damaged the intimate interrelatedness of people within and between societies. Lexicons of developed and developing economies or nations, of Western and Eastern (political or social systems), and hierarchies of primacy for languages, cultures, religions, ethnicities, economic and legal statuses, sexes, sexualities, genders, and abilities exacerbate the already dire dilemma our species faces in reimagining our relationship to the living world through which we are inextricably woven. Linda Russo and I have sought to ameliorate such illogics by inviting diverse collaborators to sketch and stretch a lexicon of connection, immersion, with-ness—though the glossary is in no sense meant to delimit approaches—to help us *imagine* ourselves inhabiting a different future than the one thus far constructed within the Anthropocene. To re-encounter the *inbetween,* we must learn not only to *resee* but also to *rearticulate* that which is seen, more complexly, anew.

As a collective endeavor, the glossary offers means of recuperative response to the challenge posed by living within, to extend Morton's term, hyperobjective systems: from geographical features (oilfields, Everglades) to planetary features (biosphere, solar system) to material constituents of earth (plutonium, Styrofoam), no less than "the sum total of all the whirring machinery of capitalism" and beyond.[9] These "objects" persist outside the compass of individual human experience, beyond human scale. Humans do not "experience" an ecosystem: though we understand that these exist, we are functionally aware of only discrete elements within such a system. A garden requires a balance of soil type, minerals, pH, light, and moisture to bring forth the harvest we have sown: yet this scant catalogue barely touches on the complex cycling of nutrients, carbon, and water, or the composite activity of climate, oceans, air currents, and landmasses generating weather patterns and precipitation or drought. Rather, the profound density of information and contiguity within the ecosystem hyperobject is accessed by humankind durationally, through the work of ecologists, biologists, geologists, physicists, and preserve managers, as well as an uncountable numbers of mundane individual encounters. As individual poets and artists seek means of engaging with the collective history of our understanding of the ecosystemic and the social-political fallout of our history with respect to it, the glossary affords durational modes of thinking, acting, and writing through the hyperobjectivity of the ecosystems and biosphere in which we are integral and fundamentally (violently) active: recuperative means of encounter with and in response to radical collectivity.

Adrienne Rich writes, "Because you still listen, because in times like these / to have you listen at all, it's necessary / to talk about trees."[10] In times like these, it is necessary to embrace the "somewhere inbetween" affording and sheltering *difference* not as distance but as *intimacy*. Deepest, inmost, intrinsic. Still the question remains, how slide sideways in thought, language, action from anthropocentric attention that privileges human needs and experience to interconnective thinking, from privileged center to radical diffusion? Experience of and connection to place afford one possible avenue. Transitional to hyperobjective reality, places serve as loci of human connection to the complex ground of our being, capable of affording access to that "somewhere inbetween" self and other, near and distant, paradoxical poles resolving moment-to-moment into contiguity. *Meeting place.* In these more local, immediate contexts, experiences of interconnection—beneficial, destructive, neutral—manifest and can be grappled with in concert with knowledge of large-scale phenomenon, each informing the another. Edward Casey articulates this relation in *The Fate of Place*: "Neither the body nor the place is a wholly determinate entity; each continually evolves, and precisely in relation to the other. The place-world is energized and transformed by the bodies that inhabit it, while these bodies are in turn guided and influenced by this world's inherent structures."[11]

Indeed, the essential and familiar homeplace nests not only within the intimate realms of household, family, neighborhood, community but within manifold hyperobjective realities, dependent on the geological history, evolutionary arcs, global weather systems, and cycling (geo)chemistries that are linked en chaine globally. While my own homeplace is an oak-and-maple-shaded drumlin on former Onondaga territory, it is also fundamentally global. Far from the warm current off the coasts of Peru and Ecuador, the warming waters of the El Niño Southern Oscillation disrupt weather here in central New York. China's carbon emissions, riding air currents between landmasses like raptors over the desert, are our carbon emissions, also riding over the earth. Rising sea levels in Louisiana, Florida, North Carolina, New Jersey, and New York City, in the Sundarbans, in the South Pacific, around the world—these crises are the natural consequences of the Industrial Revolution and the associated accumulated wealth of the United States and other First World nations. Fukushima's radiation, dispersed accidentally as a result of the catastrophic release of stored tension in the subduction zone between the oceanic Pacific Plate and the continental Okhotsk Plate, is also intimate with the landscape from which I write: each of us, *in the midst* and *inbetween*, proximate to all these hyperobjective phenomena.

Arguing that the particularity of place affords human understanding, Edward Casey suggests a rapprochement between the seemingly infinite space of relation through which life-on-this-planet exists and the specificity and intimacy of place.[12] Via immersion in the particularities of place, we may come to understand not merely our individual relationship to it but the more challenging prospect of its entanglement in the hyperobjective systems within which places are situated and within which they are implicated. The locally grown and milled organic wheat available directly from the farmer encourages agriculture suited to central New York, unbeholden to the petrochemical agricultural paradigm and affording a low-carbon footprint. Simultaneously, its increased cost and lack of easy access for purchase leave it fundamentally inaccessible to most people—unmistakable evidence of the activity of large-scale socioeconomic forces that cannot be divorced from the virtues of the project. We are *always in the midst*, local and particular, global and hyperobjective, all at once. When I purchase the grain from the farmer, not only does the bread taste astonishingly good, and not only do I build a relationship to this landscape and that farmer, whose labor feeds me; I also recognize my socioeconomic status and all that comes with it, the profound gap separating me from my near-neighbors who live just on the other side of I-81 in circumstances drastically reduced and policed, to and for whom I am responsible. All of these realities are true all at once, all demand integration into the fabric of being, thought, and action. "Ecosystemic writing" holds our multifarious paradoxes in "one mind" together, not compartmentalized nor decentering any one from all the others.

For the glossary project, in seeking out manifold insights as instigations, we hope to facilitate a body of shared experience and insight into contemporary environmental and social crises via the potency of language and literary endeavor to *bridge the gap*: from unparsed hyperobjective ecosystemic, biospheric, sociopolitical reality to intimate interpenetration. To provoke, by way of language's plasticity and potency, a proactive, functional, and indispensable shift in human awareness of our relationship to the myriad, intricate systems in which we are simultaneously enmeshed and devastatingly implicated in their, and to our, peril. A meeting place "somewhere inbetween."

Tyrone Williams, in a talk on "outsider ecopoetics" at the 2013 Conference on Ecopoetics at the University of California at

Berkeley, offers a useful key to my own address to the Anthropocene and our necessary embrace of the radical interpenetration with all life-forms and systems: "An ecopoetics worthy of its name would call itself into question indefinitely."[13] Williams charges us to embrace a "conditional orientation to a future . . . [in order to] tether the present to the future." He asserts, "The 'drag' effect—anthropocentrism—guarantees that the future remains a determined 'house' in which humans dwell and over which they lord. Is it possible to think otherwise, to imagine a future within a speculative horizon of 'freedom,' an 'outside' for that which has yet to be, and by definition, cannot be, thought?" Williams figures earthworks and bodyworks as "radical possibility for both the dislocation and relocation of languages." This glossary, we hope, will function as a "site of recuperation" in its dislocations and relocations of language. Indeed, the collaborative nature of this glossary, its authors' heterogeneous, conglomerate, diverse repurposing of terms, and/or forging of neologisms for the future corresponds to Williams's call for the ecological book "as the site of a commons, as a collective enterprise from production to distribution."

Within the drastically collective condition of life on this planet, and the unspooling, unintended consequences of the Anthropocene, this glossary offers a breadcrumb trail of language-work to follow into the future, eyes, heart, and mind open to what Williams calls "the finitude of the book[,] . . . the finitude of the human body"—each of us one body, one lifetime within the unceasing activity of the planet, all its lives and systems. Williams asks us to imagine an ecopoetics "untethered from the earth, a body no longer bounded by the concept of a globe or sphere. Imagine a body adrift from embodiment, a book, like love, unblurbed." Not *this moment* but *all* time, the accumulation of choices, unremarked and seemingly invisible. The glossary offers occasions for resistance, rethinking — re*word*ing — understanding and relationship: 135 possible instigations to visit, again and again, the extraordinary "somewhere inbetween." Archaic, destructive modes of thought, language, and action have forged a violent path through that inbetween, severing "us" from "all of us," lonely, isolate, and troubled. Language, ceaselessly mutable, extends inconstant selves through thought and into action, into the infinitely possible, permeable and mutating "somewhere inbetween."

Arthur Sze asks of the darkness, "How to live, where to go?" What answers might the glossary proffer? *Wander*. Isn't that what "we" do best? Browse the book, front to back, back to front, inside to out. Gather terms to ponder, to wander within. Or close your eyes, open the book at random, and let your finger fall upon the page. Take a term, a journal and pen, a bottle of water, and walk. Through the city, across your neighborhood, to a neighborhood new to you. Ramble through a park. Find a stream and follow its meander. Walk the woods. Sit with coffee in a strip mall, or at an open window for an hour, taking Larry Eigner for a model. Extend your vision of the city, as Ed Roberson does, holding the trees and birds, the vanished wetlands on which the city was built, in the same gaze as the shining towers soaring above. Learn to "breathe like mountains do,"[14] Joanne Kyger's lesson. Bring a campstool and sit at the margins of the city dump, where seagulls fill the air with their incongruous cries, and enormous tractors push and grade our refuse. Wonder, what did I send here this week? This year? What did I purchase, put in this ground, compressed beneath tire and blade? The dump writhes with microbes breaking down kitchen scraps, yard waste, dog manure, fast-food wrappings greasy with fat. Generating methane. What else wanders here? Who? Coyotes, stray dogs and cats, crows, folk without homes. Lives at the margins of what "we" call "home." Raccoons, owls, rats, mice, hawks, and falcons. Go camping. Walk five days, peak to peak. Return, five days running, to the same perch at a park bench, immersed in the flows eddying around you. What if we could inhabit, at last, margin and center all one? We could find ourselves, like the child in Simon Ortiz's "Canyon de Chelly," plucking up a weathered, twisty branch and knowing all at once "wood, an old root, / and around it, the earth, ourselves."[15] What it means to be here | now.

Notes

1. David George Haskell, *The Songs of Trees: Stories from Nature's Great Connectors* (Viking, 2017), 45.

2. Timothy Morton, *Ecology without Nature: Rethinking Environmental Aesthetics* (Harvard University Press, 2009), 17.

3. William Wordsworth, *The Prelude or, Growth of a Poet's Mind; an Autobiographical Poem*, (1850; PDF e-book reprint, Global Language Resources, DjVu Editions, 2001), 1 (my emphasis).

4. Timothy Morton, *Hyperobjects: Philosophy and Ecology at the End of the World* (University of Minnesota Press, 2013), 141.

5. Morton, *Ecology without Nature*, 67.

6. Morton, *Ecology without Nature*, 41.

7. Haskell, *The Songs of Trees*, 45.

8. Haskell, quoted in Ed Yong, "Trees Have Their Own Song," *Atlantic*, April 4, 2017.

9. Morton, *Hyperobjects*, 1.

10. Adrienne Rich, *Collected Poems, 1950–2012* (W. W. Norton & Company, 2016), 755.

11. Edward Casey, *The Fate of Place: A Philosophical History* (University of California Press, 1997), 414.

12. "An active desire for the particularity of place—for what is truly 'local' or 'regional'—is aroused . . . [bringing] with it the very elements shared by the planiformity of site: identity, character, nuance, history" (Casey, *The Fate of Place*, xiii).

13. Tyrone Williams, "Outsider Ecopoetics: Notes on a Problem." This talk was subsequently published in *Omniverse* (http://omniverse.us/tyrone-williams-outsider-ecopoetics/); all further quotes are from this publication.

14. Joanne Kyger, "September," in *About Now: The Collected Poems* (National Poetry Foundation, 2007), 291.

15. Simon Ortiz, *A Good Journey* (Sun Tracks, University of Arizona Press, 1984), 67.

THE CONTRIBUTORS
AND THEIR STATEMENTS

Jordan Abel is a Nisga'a writer from British Columbia and author of *Injun, Un/inhabited,* and *The Place of Scraps.* "*Earth* attempts to grapple with the expansiveness, presence, and centrality of earth, and likewise embraces unfamiliar conceptualizations of what earth is (and how we both name and interact with earth). The piece was composed out of dictionary search for the word *earth* and the subsequent related entries."

Vidhu Aggarwal grew up in the southern US and creates works in poetry, video, and scholarly writing that are oriented around cinema, transnational bodies, and digital media. "*Negative corpuscuity* came out of research into the history of Newtonian physics and quantum mechanics. For instance, Newton thought of light as a corpuscule or little body. I was curious about how the nomenclature for elementary particles became divorced from bodies—both celestial and biological—as opposed to earlier accounts. How do we revive this acute awareness of the relationship between material bodies and constituent particles?"

Kimberly Alidio, a poetry fellow at Kundiman and VONA/Voices, is the author of *After projects the resound.* "*Archive* is instigated by an email from poet Brandon Shimoda recalling the experience of reading my book-length poetry collection as a vision of the 'ruins of some kind of traumatized late-capitalist space.' To illustrate, Shimoda sent an image called 'Remains' by the Taiwanese photographer Chen Po-I, to whom the quotations at the end of my entry pertain. Chen's photograph of an abandoned 'ghost house' captures the ephemeral moment when a fishing village was relocated but before a new commercial harbor erased any trace of the villagers."

Dan Beachy-Quick is a poet and essayist who teaches in the MFA Program at Colorado State University. "*Numapen* at first seemed nonsensical but eventually came to have a strange and clear meaning to me, one pertaining much to the difficult political and environmental climate of the day."

Anna Lena Phillips Bell's work includes *Ornament, A Pocket Book of Forms*, and *Forces of Attention*; she teaches at UNC Wilmington and is editor of *Ecotone*. "*Making* suggests the bigger processes involved in how poems can come to be, how poetic practice might be seamlessly part of a life. See also the OED entry for the term. *Slow violence* helps me contemplate harms that might otherwise slip past my attention. *Attention* is a challenge I work on daily."

Mei-mei Berssenbrugge, author of twelve books of poetry including *Empathy, Four Year Old Girl, I Love Artists*, and *Hello, the Roses*, lives in northern New Mexico and New York City. Regarding *scalar, shadow*, and *witness:* "Respect is a portal."

Julia Bloch is a 2017–19 Pew Fellow in the Arts and the author of *Letters to Kelly Clarkson* and *Valley Fever*. She directs the creative writing program at the University of Pennsylvania. "*Ovulept* was coined amid research into the politics of reproductive technology. I explore how poetry can stage an argument for queer futurity even as it maintains a skeptical stance toward the violent norms of reproductive futurity. This piece thinks alongside the work of a number of theorists, including José Muñoz, Kathryn Stockton, and James Bliss, who regard futurity as a divergent sort of queer politics."

Susan Briante, author of *The Market Wonders, Pioneers in the Study of Motion*, and *Utopia Minus*, is an associate professor of creative writing at the University of Arizona. "A ruinologist since childhood in the postindustrial landscapes of central New Jersey, in grad school I wrote a dissertation titled 'American Ruins: Nostalgia, Amnesia, and Blitzkrieg Bop.' In it, I extended the definition of *ruins* to include crumbling factories, half-constructed office buildings, and abandoned storefronts to reveal how these sites offer alternative economic, social, and racial histories."

Wendy Burk is the author of *Tree Talks: Southern Arizona* and translator of Tedi López Mills's *Against the Current* and *While Light Is Built*; with M. J. Fievre, Wendy cotranslated Magela Baudoin's *Sleeping Dragons*. "**Curb cut** draws on two of the permaculture design principles articulated by David Holmgren ('Use Small and Slow Solutions' and 'Use Edges and Value the Marginal'), as well as my experience with rainwater harvesting in the Desert Southwest. Although *clasping* includes the phrase 'being with,' it's inspired not by Heidegger's 'being-with' but rather by my interest in art practices that focus on presence with/in an environment."

cris cheek most recently published *Pickles & Jams* and *down with the dabs* (in performance 2016 Cincinnati and Chicago), as poet, sound artist, and image maker. Transatlantic linguistic trickster @

Miami University, Ohio. "I'm snaggled on the *rhetoric of* **improvement**, understood as a network through which swarm other terms (like *environment*, like *swarm*, like *network*, like *profit*, like *gentrification*)."

Allison Cobb, author of *Born2, Green-Wood, Plastic: an autobiography*, and *After We All Died*, lives in Portland, Oregon, and cocurates The Switch, a reading, art, and performance series. Regarding **Anthropocene Anxiety Disorder**: "My fifteen-year-old nephew dreamed it was time to evacuate Earth. What is it like to grow up with a pervasive sense of living after the end of the future, the knowledge that one's daily activities—eating, traveling, surfing the internet—inflict wounds to home? What does that do to the nervous system? What is happiness, joy, hope in that context?"

Alicia Cohen's most recent book of poems is *Coherer*. "I am poet based in Portland, Oregon. Polluted air has been my Beatrice through the Anthropocene. Portland (after NYC and LA) has the nation's highest mortality from air as carbon dumping threatens all our ecosystems. My airshed has made me physically sick but taught me the power of an art whose medium is nothing but 'a mouthful of air' (Yeats). **Air** is spirit, song, the very interconnectedness of being. Taking a deep breath, I feel poems move us to that Paradiso future now of delicious and luscious earth potlatch."

Allison Adelle Hedge Coke's books include *The Year of the Rat, Dog Road Woman, Off-Season City Pipe, Blood Run, Burn,* and *Streaming* as well as a memoir, *Rock, Ghost, Willow, Deer*. She is the editor of the anthologies *Sing: Poetry of the Indigenous Americas, Effigies,* and *Effigies II* and is a Distinguished Professor at the University of California Riverside. Glossary contribution: ***protector***.

Christopher Cokinos is author of three books of nonfiction, including *Bodies, of the Holocene*, and an associate professor of English at the University of Arizona. "Obsessed with perceptions/ constructions of temporalities, I coined *polychronography* as a shorthand to compress my own understanding of my recent work but hope it is applicable by others to a range of work and modes of being."

Stephen Collis, author of *The Commons, On the Material*, DECOMP (with Jordan Scott), and *Once in Blockadia*, lives near Vancouver, on unceded Coast Salish Territory, and teaches at Simon Fraser University. "*Biotariat* came out of a long search for, on the one hand, a more-than-anthropocentric sense of political agency, and on the other hand, a desire to keep a sense of radical opposition, organization, and even collective 'consciousness' in our efforts to work for change (and preservation) in the name of wilderness and the 'environment.'"

Shanna Compton's books include, most recently, *The Hazard Cycle*, as well as *Brink, For Girls & Others, Down Spooky, Gamers*, and several chapbooks. "*Nomensuture* and *dysoptics* presented themselves as a pair, though *dysoptics* occurred to me first, a combination of *dystopia* and *optics* (in the political sense)."

Matthew Cooperman, author of *Spool*, and NOS (with Aby Kaupang), and other works, teaches at Colorado State University. "I've always been fascinated with landscape, view, prospect, no doubt a function of my Pacific origins, cliffside, California, deep in the iceplant; from that vantage, to a theorizing of the view. I see it in the 'clearing' of my dissertation: 'In leading us ever on and in, the poem clears a space for contemplation and action; it gathers utility as a vehicle of imminent clearing.' *Horhizome* evolves from that thinking by entering the centerless mesh, by the poem and in the world."

Brenda Coultas is the author of *The Tatters, The Marvelous Bones of Time*, and *A Handmade Museum*. "*Bluestoning* resulted from asking, 'What is this bluestone, a flat sandstone of bluish hue that once made up the sidewalks of the Hudson Valley and NYC, saying to me?'"

Jill Darling is the author of *(re)iteration(s), a geography of syntax, Solve For*, and *begin with may: a series of moments*. She teaches writing in and around southeast Michigan. Regarding *diversity*: "I'm interested in the transcendence of the limits of human possibility, in a revolution in human thought and human activity. In acknowledging our connected humanity, we have to recognize our reliance on, and reciprocal and symbiotic relationships with, other humans and species."

Sarah de Leeuw is a poet and cultural/historical geographer. Author of *Geographies of a Lover*, she believes humanities and human/ecological relationships are central to all conversations about human/nonhuman health and wellness. "*Terrotic* is part of my ongoing thinking about sexual desire as a motivating force in sustainability—thinking of nature as a lover, not a mother, to borrow from Annie Sprinkle."

Alison Hawthorne Deming's recent books are *Stairway to Heaven, Death Valley: Painted Light* (with photographer Stephen Strom), and *Zoologies: On Animals and the Human Spirit*. Regarding *sci-animism*: "I was thinking about mutualists in nature, organisms that have mutually beneficial relationships. Suddenly the word popped up. I wrote *I am a 'sci-animist'* . . . the word bubbling up from nowhere, from the same old mind that split from the apes. What I meant was that I thought science could return us to an animistic sense of the natural world, a place where transformation was expected, part of the pattern and flow."

Adam Dickinson's most recent book is *The Polymers*. He teaches poetics and creative writing at Brock University in St. Catharines, Ontario, Canada. "*Metabolic poetics* is part of an attempt to critically situate my recent work within a necessarily expanded notion of what constitutes reading and writing in the Anthropocene. Through biomonitoring and microbiome testing on my body, I am writing a book of poetry that looks at and responds to the way the 'outside' writes the 'inside' in both necessary ways (certain kinds of bacteria) and harmful ways (chemical pollution)."

Demian DinéYazhi′, a Portland-based transdisciplinary artist born to the clans Tódích'íí'nii (Bitter Water) and Naasht'ézhí Tábąąhá (Zuni Clan Water's Edge) of the Diné, is founder & director of the artist/activist initiative RISE: Radical Indigenous Survivance & Empowerment. "My work is rooted in *Radical Indigenous Queer Feminist* ideology, landscape representation, memory, HIV/AIDS-related art & activism, gender, identity, & sexuality, Indigenous survivance, & decolonization."

Thom Donovan is the author of *The Hole, Withdrawn: A Discourse*, and *Withdrawn*, and coedits and publishes ON *Contemporary Practice*. "*Use without using* owes much to the thought of Robert Kocik, for whom I edited *Supple Science: A Robert Kocik Primer* with ON Contemporary Practice. Others have traced the phrase to Augustine, Corinthians, and elsewhere."

Aja Couchois Duncan is a San Francisco Bay Area educator, coach, and writer of Ojibwe, French, and Scottish descent and author of *Restless Continent*. "Nearly a decade ago, I began a language reclamation project to learn Anishinaabemowin, the language of the Minnesota Ojibwe (Anishinaabeg). Such a process is complicated and, sometimes, painfully slow. One word that gives me great comfort is *azhigwa*, the Ojibwe temporal adverb for now, as in now, just now, already."

Camille T. Dungy is the author, most recently, of *Trophic Cascade* (poems) and the essay collection *Guidebook to Relative Strangers*, as well as editor of *Black Nature: Four Centuries of African American Nature Poetry*. "Both my terms (**radical empathy** and **torpor**) are real words, reimagined in light of the needs of our day."

Marcella Durand's latest books are *Rays of the Shadow* and *Le Jardin de M. (Garden of M.)*, translated by Olivier Brossard in a bilingual edition. "Attributed to the Breton poet, Eugène Guillevic, **terraqué** signifies a complicated and, to my mind, trembling existence between earth and water."

Alec Finlay is an artist and poet whose recent publications include *A Variety of Cultures, ebban an' flowan, a better tale to tell, Global Oracle*. "**Conspectus**, **path**, and **place-name** arose from a concern with place-awareness, and an ongoing interest in the Dictionary definition—a form that still has its uses."

Forrest Gander's recent books include *Redstart: An Ecological Poetics* (with John Kinsella) and *Core Samples from the World*. "A clade is a group of organisms (like us) believed to have evolved from a common ancestor. **Reconstructive cladistics** might be a way of rebranching relationships, recuperating some sense of our connectedness to other species very different from us (like trilobites, which have the features—cephalon, pygidium, glabella—mentioned in the redefinition), a way of delimiting amending the perception of human beings as disconnected from (or superior to) all other forms of life."

Suzi F. Garcia, poetry editor at Noemi Press, has had work featured in *Vinyl, The Offing,* DREGINALD, *Reservoir Journal*, and more. Regarding **sus-ten-ance**: "I've been rethinking survival beyond just our own action, but how we are supported, by our community, by our earth. We are not just living, but we are being given life. There are times when I barely feel able to enact life, but I am sustained anyway."

Arielle Greenberg's recent books include *Come Along with Me to the Pasture Now* and *Locally Made Panties*. She is coauthor with Rachel Zucker of *Home/Birth: A Poemic* and coeditor with Becca Klaver of *Electric Gurlesque*. Regarding **inanimals** and **unanimals**: "I have identified as a primate since childhood. Years ago while at an artists' colony, a bunch of us went to a local theater to see the Charlie Kaufman/Michel Gondry film *Human Nature,* which renewed/revived my lifelong interest in the animalness of our primate species."

Roberto Harrison's books include *Os, Counter Daemons, bicycle, culebra, Bridge of the World,* and *Yaviza.* He is Milwaukee's poet laureate for 2017–19, a visual artist, and a Tec Panamanian nationalist. "I am from Panamá, hence my entry on what **Panamá** might mean. I also feel fortunate to have encountered **Saloma**, a practice very distinctive to Panamá. My entry on the **Tecumseh Republic** is based on my poem by the same name included at the end of my book, *Yaviza*. That piece is partly how I've managed to begin to feel at home in some ways in this country despite its horrors."

j/j hastain is the inventor of The Mystical Sentence Projects and author of cross-/trans-genre books *libertine monk, The Non-Novels,* and *The Xyr Trilogy: A Metaphysical Romance of Experimental Realisms.* Regarding *the deep*: "The first time I felt her sea foam inside me I did not know it was the Inuit goddess, Sedna. She had knocked me out from within me. Months of watery haunting, of bibliomancy and revelation gave me her name, her story, and some of her desires. Seeing the edges of mother ocean from above, the salting slam of her, clarified Sedna's longtime teaching. Pelagic feminisms so mysterious it seems they might not be of this world very much are. She remade me."

jared hayes is the author of *go with me, the dead love,* and *Bandit.* Jared is a cofounder of livestock editions and *summer stock.* "(bolded): i discover the term *temenos* listening to the Naropa Archives of Robert Duncan Lectures, then receive a pamphlet in the mail: in the introduction Ammiel Alcalay describes the early influence temenos has for Robert Duncan and Charles Olson's relationship; (italics): listening to Philip Whalen, i hear him describe the academy as a walking grove of trees, then i superimpose the term *sacred*, conflating arboretum, academy, and temenos; (bold italics): Emily Dickinson wrote these words onto an envelope held in her pocket; sitting in an arboretum; i pull them out of my own pocket, transmitcommuning."

Brenda Hillman is the author of nine collections of poetry. Regarding *crypto-animist activism*: "Many years ago i started realizing spiritual life & activism are not separate. Individualized presences come along in any action, experienced as a granular particulate. For example, i teach at Saint Mary's College, where i participate in a weekly vigil. Some of us stand or dance under a live oak while people walk by. While we hold up the signs, other beings as microbes join us under the tree, Blake or Baraka . . . *We have no proof that they don't . . . When the time comes, some will rise & some will dance & some will lay our bodies down.*"

Angela Hume is the author of *Middle Time* and the chapbooks *Melos, The Middle,* and *Second Story of Your Body,* and coeditor of *Ecopoetics: Essays in the Field.* "**Ecolyric** was composed with gestures toward terms and/or writings of Sara Ahmed, Jonathan Bate, William Blake, Grace Cho, G. W. F. Hegel, Myung Mi Kim, Audre Lorde, Andreas Malm, Claudia Rankine, Jed Rasula, Muriel Rukeyser."

Brenda Iijima has authored seven collections of poetry, including *Remembering Animals,* and serves as editor of Portable Press at Yo-Yo Labs. "I register *relaxation time* emotionally and somatically, which, to me, underlines how human animals often can't surmise the threatening effects of a crisis that has to do with coexistence as shared time and space. An ongoing death event of this magnitude encompasses everyone, all life. As Thom Van Dooren writes in *Extinction Studies: Stories of Time, Death, and Generations,* 'Coevolution can switch over into coextinction; co-becoming into entangled patterns of dying-with.' This term is a pertinent metaphor for our times."

Megan Kaminski, author of two books of poetry, *Deep City* and *Desiring Map,* is an assistant professor in the University of Kansas's

Creative Writing Program and curates the Taproom Poetry Series. "My thinking about **permeability** is part of a larger project to revision the lyric to support a self composed by commingling and collaboration, a self that resists the transcendent solitude that we tend to associate with the contemporary lyric mode as shaped by its lineage out of the 'Romantic lyric,' a self that can become site for transformation. This exploration is grounded in research in plant and animal studies, epigenetic inheritance, and phenomenology."

Bhanu Kapil is the author of five collections of prose/poetry, most recently *Ban en Banlieue*. "The definition of **ecobereavement** reloops and startles me. Reading it, two years on, makes me feel like a human being, though what it contains is an ex-human view. The genesis of the term was that I was visiting Delhi in Fall 2014, looking out the taxi window on the long journeys, that sometimes took five hours, across one of the most polluted cities on the planet."

Sonnet L'Abbé, PhD and author of *A Strange Relief, Killarnoe*, and *Sonnet's Shakespeare*, is a professor of creative writing and English at Vancouver Island University. "My doctoral dissertation looked at how the American poet Ronald Johnson used Romantic plant metaphors to represent modernist mindedness, ecosensitivity, and utopic vision. I found I needed words like **phytosentience** just to have language to discuss what he was getting at."

Christine Leclerc is the author of *Oilywood* and *Counterfeit*, and an editor of *The Enpipe Line: 70,000+ km of poetry written in resistance to the Northern Gateway pipeline proposal* and *portfolio milieu*. She lives in Burnaby / Coast Salish Territories and is training as a climatologist. "**Echoherence** describes localized, fleeting wholes formed by beings and objects or traces. The pronunciation draws on the prefix *eco-* as the link to ecology conveys relationship between space and beings. The spelling of the prefix, *echo*, is also important as without sound source or space there is no echo, yet combination generates a whole."

Dana Teen Lomax is a northern California writer (*Currency, Disclosure*, and other works), editor (including *Kindergarde*), and activist. "The constructed word *vivitocracy* contains the Latin roots *viv* and *vit*, which mean 'alive' and 'life,' respectively. Vivitocracy also contains the Greek suffix *-cracy*, meaning 'rule.' The word, then, is akin to 'the bond of life.' Vivitocracy suggests that when consciousness is heightened by dire circumstance, we necessarily overcome our pettiness, help each other out, and recognize the value of all life forms mutually—outside of capital or external systems. Thus, given the global environmental crisis, ours is an incredibly promising moment."

Gerry Loose, a poet, both on the page and by ephemeral/permanent inscription in landscapes, his latest books are *An Oakwoods Almanac, fault line, night exposures*, and *A Great Book of the Woods*. "That places come to us and not we to them is *way-dwelling*. The familiar with no time. We are what finds us. I often don't know what things mean. In way-dwelling they tell me & I wake for an instant into the great fold of knowing."

Jill Magi is the author of five books, including *Labor*, and several chapbooks, including *Sign Climacteric*. "This is how *climacteric* came to me: in the middle of hormonal shifts, recalibrating the energy of giving, work, mortality. I could go sour or choose to ripen. I went into poetry, began meditating, and the earth said, 'I'm at a critical juncture also.' This entry gathers several sources including the Estonian origins story: a giant woman sits in a bath, the Baltic Sea, balancing an egg on her knee just for fun until it rolls off, breaks, and the pieces form land."

Eric Magrane is coeditor of *The Sonoran Desert: A Literary Field Guide* and founding editor of *Spiral Orb*. His recent work appears in *Big Energy Poets: Ecopoetry Thinks Climate Change* and *Creativity* (Key Ideas in Geography Series). Regarding **geopoetics**: "I often think about my poetics as a geographic practice, and my work in human and cultural geography as a poetic practice. My relationship to **bycatch** has emerged out of an ongoing art-science research project with marine conservationist Maria Johnson, in which I have spent nights aboard shrimp trawlers in Mexico's Gulf of California, knee-deep in writhing fish pulled up from the benthic zone."

E. J. McAdams, author of TRANSECTS and *4x4*, is a poet, artist, and collaborator who lives in Harlem, Ward's Island Sewershed, Manhattan, Lower Hudson Watershed, New York, USA, Earth. "From the moment I became a park ranger in populous New York City, I was fascinated by the concept of a **desire line** and its ecological, spiritual, collective, democratic, topological and ethical implications. There is so much desire in our world, and it extends beyond our species. Where will it all go?"

David James Miller is the author most recently of CANT. He edits *Elis Press and SET*, a biennial journal of innovative writing. "***Echolocution***'s genesis reflects the influence of 'echolocation,' a term used to describe sound-based locative techniques performed by bats and other organisms. The term also recalls the 'eco' of ecological attention and writing, as well as the stylistic 'locution' found in the personal, material characteristics of a writer's work. Other influences include Pauline Oliveros's notion of *Deep Listening* in performance and the Onkyōmusicians' shared techniques and emphasis on silence during performance, especially in its earliest iterations."

Rusty Morrison is the author of *Beyond the Chainlink, After Urgency, the true keeps calm biding its story, Book of the Given,* and *Whethering,* and copublisher of Omnidawn. "Both *burrowing* and *repoise* arrived as surprise in a period of challenging pressures; they were initially provocations, or what I have come to understand as opportunities to glimpse a narrowing, even suffocating, limitation that I hadn't realized held me hostage. Both of these 'coinages' were of a new currency, and in them is a strong current, electric with the force of an altered ideation, richly affect driven, and freeing."

Lori Anderson Moseman's latest poetry collections are *Flash Mob, All Steel,* and *Full Quiver,* a collaboration with book artist Karen Pava Randall. "*Animacy* is an ongoing conversation with poet Meredith Stricker, author of *Our Animal.* Our walks and talks inhabit California's central coast—site of the 2016 Soberanes Fire and the 2017 bombogenesis pundits call Lucifer. Our shared reading practice seeks solace, kinship, alienation, abeyance, breath, space, and light, so she says in 'Why Not the Forest.'"

Camilla Nelson is a language artist and researcher based in southwest England. She is author of *Apples and Other Languages* and *A Yarn Er Narrative* and editor of Singing Apple Press. "I'm interested in language-making as world-making, a distributed intra-activity between a vast range of elements, organisms and forces (known and unknown). *Metaform* and *page-making* offer particular ways of understanding language-making as a material force that constitutes and engenders our world's continuing emergence."

Denise Newman, author of *Future People* and translator of *Baboon,* by Danish writer Naja Marie Aidt, teaches at the California College of the Arts. **Hazel White,** author of *Peril as Architectural Enrichment* and *Vigilance Is No Orchard,* is an editor at University of California Department of Agriculture and Natural Resources. "Together we completed, in 2016, a two-year site project, *Biotic Portal at Strawberry Creek* (bioticportal.com), a collaboration with the UC Botanical Garden, at Berkeley. *Dispersal* arrived as we detailed the animations in the garden and tested imagination as a force of movement."

Hoa Nguyen's poetry collections include *As Long as Trees Last, Red Juice, Poems 1998–2008,* and *Violet Energy Ingots.* Regarding *recovery* and *resistance*: "A root-ball formed for me in a Poetics Seminar in Sante Fe, New Mexico, as we confronted questions on how to re-vision, practice, and study alternatives to 'a contemporary political imagination framed by the settler-colonial and antiblack regulations of liberal humanity.' This study produced a provocative 'Question Manifesto' that expanded sideways, upward, and downward for me (like a root system) in my ongoing studies, workshops, and conversations. Reference materials include studies of rhizomes, weeds, and the practice of art as a mode of resistance with ethical responsibilities."

Mónica Teresa Ortiz, born and raised in the Texas Panhandle, is a Macondo fellow, and coeditor of the SFA Press anthology *Pariahs*; her first poetry collection is *muted blood.* "***Bordered*** means along an edge, to be adjacent to, or, perhaps most acutely, to be close to an extreme. On the physical border of Texas and Mexico, the political demarcation that requires papers to cross but no poets to build a wall, is simply an illusionary practice, a symbolic showing of decorum. In other words, the border exists because we allow it to exist—just like the starving dogs."

Danielle Pafunda, author of seven books, including *The Dead Girls Speak in Unison*, *Natural History Rape Museum*, and *Beshrew That Heart That Makes My Heart to Groan*, lives in the desert with her children. "The term *viral avatar* germinates from the obsession of the human host with eliminating the virus while simultaneously blithely coding itself into all the earth's materials with often devastating result."

Gillian Parrish is an assistant professor in the MFA writing program at Lindenwood University. Her book *of rain and nettles wove* is forthcoming from Singing Horse Press in 2018. Her work has appeared in various journals, including *Gulf Coast* and *Volt*, *Earthlines* and *ecozon@*. She curates *spacecraftproject*, a journal of arts and literature. Her entry, *woveness*, "originally bristled with hyperlinks (form fitting content) from 'tendril' to *tendrel*'s Tibetan definition of interdependent arising, from 'suture' to *sutra* (threads in a woven text), from 'root' to Lewis Thomas's essay digging (in both senses) the roots of language."

Craig Santos Perez, a native Chamorro from the Pacific Island of Guam, is the author of three books and a participating scholar in the Asia-Pacific Observatory Environmental Humanities project. He teaches courses on eco-poetry at the University of Hawai'i, Manoa. "*Indigenous ecopoetics* came from my study of native poetries about the environment, as well from my own experience as an Indigenous writer."

John Pluecker, a writer, translator, interpreter, artist, and co-founder with Jen Hofer of Antena, is the author of *Ford Over* and has translated numerous books from the Spanish, including *Antígona González*. "**IOYAIENE** is a word that has become endlessly necessary for me, a word I need to repeat and to re-enunciate over and over again, reminding myself constantly that colonial processes have robbed us of both its meaning and its original soundings."

Deborah Poe has authored numerous books of poetry, including *keep* and *Elements*. "Robert Macfarlane's writing in the *Guardian*, Glenn Albrecht's 2007 study on **solastalgia**, and Kate MacDowell's porcelain sculpture *Solastalgia* all moved me to draft a piece exploring the idea and then to collaborate with transmedia artist Hassen Saker on a short poetry film."

Chris Pusateri is the author of ten titles, most recently *Common Time*. "**Protext** arises at the confluence of creativity and doubt. It concerns the age-old question of how poetry helps advance social justice without becoming doctrinaire. It's hard to know how literature might be weaponized, how it might act in concert with other forces to bring about progressive change, particularly when we consider the terrifying economies of scale that stand opposite us. *In concert* is crucial, because literature without allies cannot move the needle in a country where nearly a third of people did not read a book last year."

a rawlings is a poet and interdisciplinary artist. Her books include *Wide slumber for lepidopterists*, *o w n*, and *si tu*. "My methods over the past fifteen years have foregrounded sensual poetries, vocal and contact improvisation, theater of the rural, and conversations with landscapes. My neologism *að jökla* is part of a larger ecopoethic exploration of abiotic entities including Icelandic glaciers and North Atlantic sediment."

Anna Reckin, based in England and schooled in the US (University of Minnesota, University at Buffalo), her work is published in the UK and internationally. "*Inter-strand* for me is primarily about process: recognition of rubbliness, of layers that tumble into one another, over time or through violent rupture; and the connections that nonetheless arise and persist. Included in it are sparks of anger and resistance. I see *inter-strand* played out in prose fiction, too, in Ruth Ozeki's *A Tale for the Time Being*, for example, or Ali Smith's *How to Be Both*."

Marthe Reed (1959–2018), author most recently of *Nights Reading*, and the ecopoetic chapbooks *Data Primer, a transparent reality*, and *Florula Ludoviciana*, published Black Radish Books. "*Ecopoethos* makes explicit the necessary interpolation of ethics, making, and ecology-as-home. The term *t/here* pushes toward a sense of time and place that manifest multidimensionally, past-present-future, near-middle-far, (re)asserting the fundamental interconnectedness of being."

Evelyn Reilly has written three books that attempt to manifest a poetics of the Anthropocene: *Styrofoam, Apocalypso*, and *Echolocation*. "I contemplated the idea of **unpersonism** while writing the essay 'Vulcan Feminist Poetics,' an exploration of the gender dynamics of science-inspired poetry. In addition to its feminist preoccupations, Vulcan Poetics proposes many arenas of poetic investigation including: multiple language worlds; material being (aesthetics, erotics, ethics), unpersonism, and the technological sublime."

Mg Roberts, a Kundiman Fellow and VONA/Voices alum, is author of *Anemal Uter Meck* and *not so, sea*, and coedited *Nests and Strangers: On Asian Women Poets*. "In **bearing** I wanted to archive the way landscapes and bodies aren't distinctive of quality, but rather in oscillation. Like nature, the body keeps moving, is never stable, especially in terms of context and its relation to violence. The embodiment of the lode on one's person and the grouping of space—submissions a body/landscape must undergo to frame or enact on. As that to bear."

Erin Robinsong is a poet, performance maker, and the author of *Rag Cosmology*. "My work explores intimate dimensions of ecology, where the personal is ecological and the ecological is personal. I look at the way environmental rhetoric and language make it difficult to think and respond to ecological danger with the level of urgency we do for other forms of danger—a car crash, a fire, a terrorist threat. As a corrective to the notion of the environment as 'out there,' I wanted a word to describe the radical closeness we actually experience—omnitouch? intertouch? hapticosm? **Geohaptics**."

Lee Ann Roripaugh, author of four volumes of poetry, most recently *Dandarians,* and currently South Dakota's poet laureate. "**Empiricism** addresses the fraught feedback loop between nature and technology. Much of our scientific curiosity of the world has gone hand in hand with empire—including the colonizing impulse to collect, categorize, classify, and 'master.' A strange irony is that science and empirical knowledge are key to both recognizing and understanding climate change and ecological destruction, and to preserving, mitigating, conserving dwindling ecological resources. This feedback loop between nature and technology leads me to wonder whether scientific repair is hubristic intervention, or an organic, potentially redemptive development of (human) nature."

Linda Russo, author most recently of *Participant* and *To Think of Her Writing Awash in Light,* lives in the inland northwestern US. "*Bodyregionalism, everyhere,* and **inhabitant,** because crucial to belong to, to be of, and to value geographical places no matter how seemingly unromantic or uninteresting or unlovable. By such means enter into, because already within, the conflicts that, as a continual process, mark, modify, and define place."

Lisa Samuels is a transnational writer and sound artist whose recent books are *Tender Girl, Over Hear, A TransPacific Poetics* (edited with Sawako Nakayasu), and *Symphony for Human Transport.* "*Distributed centrality* came to me in pondering how to describe the ethical and political necessity of viewing everything as value-equal. Apparently, power is seductive, othering is ubiquitous, and hierarchy is omnivorous. If we're really postcolonial and global and transhuman, then reinventing language is part of shaping anew the political everyday, making more decisions like the 2017 legal personhood status accorded to the Whanganui River."

Cheryl Savageau is a French/Abenaki poet, writer, former biology teacher, and author of *Dirt Road Home, Mother/Land* and the children's book, *Muskrat Will Be Swimming.* Regarding **akiw8gon, Land,** and **reciproesis.** "I was raised by a lake in central Massachusetts. In first grade, the teacher asked us if water is alive, and I enthusiastically answered yes! But she said no, it's not—my first experience of cultural dissonance. Abenaki is a language of verbs, of process. There are words in Abenaki that have taken me a whole poem to express in English."

Jennifer Scappettone's books include the cross-genre verse works *From Dame Quickly* and *The Republic of Exit 43: Outtakes & Scores from an Archaeology and Pop-Up Opera of the Corporate Dump*. "Seeking to redefine **archaeology** in terms of language, landscape, and the history of affect has been part of my practice since I embarked on a Greco-Roman excavation at Morgantina twenty-five years ago; I encountered **overburden** and **orridi** in dredging up the history of copper mining, electrification, and the material rain of the cloud. **Pathmaking** emerged from collaborating on movement and text scores at Fresh Kills Landfill for the performance project PARK."

Kate Schapira, author of *Handbook for Hands That Alter as We Hold Them Out*, and (with Erika Howsare) *FILL: A Collection*. She runs the Publicly Complex Reading Series and offers climate anxiety counseling. "Before understanding **communication** in this way, I read *Braiding Sweetgrass* by Robin Wall Kimmerer, *Annihilation* by Jeff VanderMeer, and an article about trees speaking together underground. I walked in the woods with my friend, watered my houseplants, and listened to people's anxieties—this is how I communicate now, even though I was doing it, already, the whole time."

Andrew Schelling's recent books include *Tracks Along the Left Coast: Jaime de Angulo and Pacific Rim Culture, From the Arapaho Songbook* and *A Possible Bag* (both poetry), and the anthology *Love and the Turning Seasons: India's Poetry of Spiritual and Erotic Longing*. "**Game trail** comes from my own high country experience. I follow the long-used tracks of large mammals, which regularly show the best routes across rough territory. A study of Colorado's Paleoindians backs this up. **Neséíhi** came out of my encounter with earlier languages of the High Plains–Rocky Mountain interface.

Persecuted or endangered languages still work: 'user manuals' for specific bioregions."

Susan M. Schultz is author, most recently, of two volumes of *Dementia Blog*, and three of *Memory Cards*, as well as *A Poetics of Impasse in Modern and Contemporary American Poetry*, and founder of Tinfish Press. "Sources for *shelter*: the *Honolulu Star-Advertiser*, the *Civil Beat*, the Institute for Human Services website, the *Oxford English Dictionary*, the National Park Service, the Catholic News Agency, the Fast Company website."

Brenda Sieczkowski has published the chapbooks *Wonder Girl in Monster Land* and *Fallout and Flotation Devices* and *Like Oysters Observing the Sun*, a full-length poetry collection. Originally from Nebraska, she currently lives and writes in Salt Lake City, Utah. "Heavily developed for cropland, the Great Plains region is a highly endangered ecosystem. *The Great Plaints* imagines species dissonance created by displacement of native plants as a type of extended echoic memory (auditory haunting), ghost echoes looping interference from past and potential (posthuman) landscapes."

Eleni Sikelianos, author of eight books of poetry, most recently *Make Yourself Happy*, and two hybrid memoirs (most recently *You Animal Machine)*, has taught poetry in public schools, homeless shelters, and prisons, and collaborates frequently with other artists. "*Phylogeny* comes from my current poetry work, which looks into the open from our deep animal past, allowing passage backward and forward in worlds and in times, tapping on our structural heritage."

Jonathan Skinner, author of *Political Cactus Poems, Birds of Tifft, Chip Calls*, and *Warblers* and founding editor of *ecopoetics*, teaches at the University of Warwick. "Righteousness around **walking** feels precious. Yet grow into footsteps: you'll learn from them. Want to know a place? Walk. No need for life-changing adventures. Crawling is even better (says E. Abbey). Born and raised in a midsize town, walking's how I got to know cities. I bicycled up and down mountains, owned a car in my thirties. Carless now, I walk and use public transport. In my teaching, yes, the walk is on the test."

Carmen Gimenez Smith, author of *Post-Identity*, editor of *Angels of the Americlypse* with John Chavez, and publisher of Noemi Press. "*South borderland* was an attempt to write about the landscape I lived in for the past fifteen years (southern New Mexico) and how it intersects with my identity as a US citizen with brown skin."

Jessica Smith, founding editor of *Foursquare* and *name* magazines and Coven Press, is author of *Organic Furniture Cellar* and *Life-List*. Regarding **odontomancy**. "A tornado watch in Alabama, my worries about the safety of our school's resident chickens, inspired research on alectryomancy. I learned that unlike other birds, chickens can still form teeth. I wondered: What environmental conditions might cause this ancient part of their genetic code to activate again? What might the presence or absence of animal teeth predict?"

Jared Stanley, the author of three books—*EARS*, *The Weeds*, and *Book Made of Forest*—lives in Reno, Nevada. "I count myself among those who think of poetry as a grand waste place, like a **ditch**. Ditches can always be put to dramatic use—you can hide stuff in a ditch. It was fun, as a child, to find scraps and fragments in ditches—photographs and letters, the more decayed the better, hints and rotted emblems. Images and letters decayed there. So exciting. Junk juts above the water, green and hairy with algae."

Heidi Lynn Staples is author of four collections, including *A**A*A*A*. With the poet Amy King, she has coedited *Poets for Living Waters* and the recently released *Big Energy Poets: Ecopoetry Thinks Climate Change*. Regarding **B-RAD (Bioregional Attachment Disorder)**: "I've begun asking myself how I can foster attachment to place, to heal from the trauma of perpetual dislocation. I've arrived at an embodied artistic practice in which I apply the poetics of the 'necropastoral' (Joyelle McSweeney) and 'enchantment' (Jane Bennett) to write as part of getting myself outside, walking daily, hiking, and sleeping on the ground across the Mobile Bay–Tennesaw Watershed."

Eleni Stecopoulos is the author of *Visceral Poetics, Daphnephoria*, and *Armies of Compassion*. She teaches in the San Francisco Bay Area. "**Sanctuary** meditates on different locations, from the ancient Greek *temenos* (precinct) to the contemporary sanctuary movement for undocumented immigrants in the US and the struggle to protect the sacred site of the Ohlone Shellmound in West Berkeley, California. **Geopathy** redirects environmental sensitivity, explored in an earlier essay by the same title in *Visceral Poetics*."

Eileen Tabios is the author of *Love in a Time of Belligerence* and other works, editor of *Galatea Resurrects (A Poetry Engagement)*, and publisher of Meritage Press. "I thought of **cloudygenous** for reflecting the contemporary integration of internet access into daily living, a practice more likely to deepen and expand in the future. Indigeneity historically is tied to the land. As human population continues to rise and becomes more dense in places, access to land may become less common, even as the internet's reach expands. Those already born and likely to be born into such an environment are likely to create a new type of culture."

Brian Teare is the author of five books, most recently *The Empty Form Goes All the Way to Heaven*. An associate professor at Temple University, he lives in South Philadelphia. "Basic bioregional literacy includes knowing where our drinking water comes from, how it arrives at our taps and toilets, and where wastewater goes afterward. Our water systems are most often built on and feed back into our **watershed**s, the preexisting hydrological features of a given bioregion. The history and logistics of Philadelphia's water supply have taught me a great deal about the intricate way industries, ecosystems, and human bodies intertwine in the Anthropocene."

Melissa Tuckey is author of *Tenuous Chapel*, a cofounder of Split This Rock, and editor of *Ghost Fishing: An Eco-Justice Poetry Anthology*. "I come to the term **Eco-Justice Poetry** through my work as an editor of *Ghost Fishing*. The anthology began out of my own desire, as both an activist and poet, for an ecopoetry that speaks to the social, political, and economic complexity of environmental crisis."

Kevin Varrone lives in Philadelphia, where he organizes the annual small press festival, *Philalalia*. "*Thereoir* relates to how language visible in cities speaks to the character of those cities. Infatuated by how graffiti artists blanket a neighborhood, I started paying attention to paint markings on the streets in Philadelphia as well — symbols indicating infrastructure work to be done. It appeared as a kind of legal graffiti, a private language that I could see but not understand, which began to feel like the wine industry's concept of terroir, the mystical specificity of land, earth, and climate of a geographical region that marks the wine produced there."

Divya Victor, author of *Kith*, unsub, and *Things to Do with Your Mouth*, she has been a citizen of three nation-sites of the Tamilian diaspora — India, Singapore, and the usa — which led to the concept of the sari as a zone of cleaving, as reflected in *skirt* and *unskirt*.

Danielle Vogel, a cross-genre writer and ceremonialist who grew up on the south shore of Long Island and author of *Between Grammars*, the artist book *Narrative and Nest*, and the chapbooks *In Resonance* and *lit*. "My entries (***bodied, language, reassociated, repair***) were born from a deeply embodied writing practice. I compose at the threshold where writing meets ceremony. I imagine these redefinitions as invocations that might be recited when needing nourishment, a heightened and healthful awareness of the self, a reminder of the synergetic communion of all things."

Asiya Wadud is a poet and second-grade teacher living in Brooklyn, New York. She is the author of *crosslight for youngbird* and the chapbook *we, too, are but the fold*. "In my work, I probe what it means to make and unmake borders, as well as the expression of borders: mother tongue, language and mastery, and citizenship and nationality. I am also interested in how these notions are expressed in the natural world. ***Archipelagos,*** by definition, acknowledge the islands beyond one's own island, whereas ***atolls*** can remain self-contained if they really want to."

Fred Wah, author of *Diamond Grill, Faking It: Poetics and Hybridity*, and *Scree: The Collected Earlier Poems 1962–1991*, studied music, literature, and linguistics at the University of British Columbia and at SUNY at Buffalo. "***Betweenness*** derives from my interest in racial hybridity, an increasingly poignant attention as such matters as indigeneity, colonization, and immigration, claim more discursive sites. 'Trans-'ing hyphenation to a geographical address sustains a poetics of the personal and, thus, the local. The poems in my book *is a door* is one place where I've worked on those ideas."

Anne Waldman, author of over forty books, including *The Iovis Trilogy, Voice's Daughter of a Heart Yet to Be Born*, and *Manatee/Humanity*, is cofounder with Allen Ginsberg of Naropa University's Jack Kerouac School of Disembodied Poetics. *Orakinzop* is offered "*with gratitude to* CTR, CR, GR, *dharma teachers of past & to come.*"

Hazel White, author of *Peril as Architectural Enrichment* and *Vigilance Is No Orchard*, is an editor at University of California Department of Agriculture and Natural Resources. **Denise Newman**, author of *Future People* and translator of *Baboon*, by Danish writer Naja Marie Aidt, teaches at the California College of the Arts. "Together we completed, in 2016, a two-year site project, *Biotic Portal at Strawberry Creek* (bioticportal.com), a collaboration with the UC Botanical Garden, at Berkeley. *Dispersal* arrived as we detailed the animations in the garden and tested imagination as a force of movement."

Tyrone Williams teaches literature and theory at Xavier University in Cincinnati, Ohio, and is the author of five books of poetry, *c.c., On Spec, The Hero Project of the Century, Adventures of Pi, Howell*, and the companion chapbooks *Between Red and Green: The Black Brigade of Cincinnati* and *Red between Green*. "*Washland* is a neologism conceived by independent scholar Pat Clifford and me in reference to the collaborative project we completed in 2016 (that became the poem *washpark*) analyzing the political, economic, and social repercussions attending the gentrification of a public park (Washington Park) located in downtown Cincinnati."

Laura Woltag is the author of *Hush Hyletics*; her recent poetic projects wonder toward watching, usually within the various habitats and cultures of the SF Bay Area. "*Weave watching* arises from my exploration of the senses and the varieties of sense perceptions available to the human animal. As a poet, for a long time I privileged sonic noticing over the visual. The visual seemed so easily manipulated via material culture into an extension of grasping and possessing. So what does it mean to watch with, to reclaim sight for relation that informs instinct and interconnection?"

Elisabeth Workman, author of *Endlessness Is No Desolation, Ultramegaprairieland*, and numerous chapbooks, lives in Minneapolis, where she cocurates the Next Poetix Reading Series at Minneapolis College of Art and Design. "This neologism, ***betwixtuation***, surfaced while thinking/writing about Agnes Varda's *Les glaneurs et la glaneuse* in a longer messay on chance, margins, and the encounter between Baubo and Demeter—a poetics in which we might be gleaners of/in a betwixtuation (betwixtuationists?)."

Maged Zaher was born in Cairo and currently lives in Atlanta. His collected poems appeared in 2017. Regarding ***The Other***: "Since I started writing in English, I was invited to many poetry readings to discuss 'othering.' I was sometimes introduced literally as a representative of the other. Now, I'm simply not interested in being an other, nor in that concept as a whole. I found the roots of accepting the term 'other' in humanism, where I started intellectually: specifically from 'all humans are created equal.' I believe now that humanism is a deeply flawed position that leads to the obliteration of animals and the planet. I am looking for a weird balance between Althusserian structuralism and environmentalism."

INDEX

Page numbers in **boldface** refer to glossary entries, identified also by entry headword, also in **boldface**. Page numbers in *italics* refer to the editors' introduction and afterword.

About the Editors

LINDA RUSSO is the author of several books of poetry, including *Participant* (Lost Roads Press, 2016), winner of the Bessmilr Brigham Poets Prize, and *To Think of her Writing Awash in Light* (Subito Press, 2016), a collection of lyrical essays. Scholarly essays have appeared in *Among Friends: Engendering the Social Site of Poetry* (University of Iowa Press) and other edited collections. She teaches creative writing at Washington State University and lives in the inland northwestern US.

MARTHE REED (1959–2018) is the author of five books, including *Nights Reading* (Lavender Ink, 2014), *(em)bodied bliss* (Moria Books, 2013), and the collaborative *Pleth* (Unlikely Books, 2013), with j hastain. She was co-publisher and managing editor for Black Radish Books, and her poems have appeared in *Jacket2*, *Tarpaulin Sky*, and *New American Writing*, among other publications.